THE
ROAD RUNNER'S
GUIDE TO
NEW YORK CITY

THE ROAD RUNNER'S GUIDE TO NEW YORK CITY

by Patti Hagan
with Joe Cody

Maps by George Colbert

Times
BOOKS

ACKNOWLEDGEMENTS

For their help, en route, we would like to thank: Fred Lebow, president of the New York Road Runners Club, Joe Kleinerman, Ted Corbitt, William and Paul Bengtson of Inwood Hill Park, Molly and Harry Colgan (runner-readers), Ben Grundstein, Schellie Hagan (running writing critic), Art Hall, Richie Innamorato, Bob Orazem, Ed Quinlan, Dr. Norb Sander, Hugh Sweeny, Pete Whitehouse of Tottenville High School, Cahit Yeter, Connie Stallings of *Audubon*, Elizabeth Macklin of *The New Yorker*, Mary Evans our literary running agent, and our marathon editor, Patrick Filley.

Patti Hagan
Joe Cody

Grateful acknowledgement is made to the New York Road Runners Club for permission to reprint the text of The New York City Marathon chapter, which previously appeared in slightly different form as part of THE NEW YORK CITY MARATHON PROGRAM.
Copyright ©1978, The New York Road Runners Club.

Book design by Bliem Kern
Maps by George Colbert.

Published by TIMES BOOKS, a division
of Quadrangle/The New York Times Book Co., Inc.
Three Park Avenue, New York, N.Y. 10016

Published simultaneously in Canada by
Fitzhenry & Whiteside, Ltd., Toronto

Library of Congress Cataloging in Publication Data
Hagan, Patti.
The road runner's guide to New York City.
1. Running—New York (City)—Guide-books.
2. New York (City)—Description—1951.
—Guide-books. I. Cody, Joe. II. Title.
GV1061.22. N71133   1979   917.47'.1   79-66840
ISBN 0-8129-0867-8
Manufactured in the United States of America.

CONTENTS

FOREWORD by Fred Lebow   7

INTRODUCTION how to use this book   8

NEW YORK CITY MARATHON   12

MANHATTAN Central Park...Riverside Park...   20
Harlem River–High Bridge...Fort Tryon
Park–Cloisters...Inwood Hill Park...
East River...Roosevelt Island...Battery–
Brooklyn Bridge–Westside Highway...
Manhattan Mini-Runs

BROOKLYN Prospect Park...Coney Island–Sheepshead   46
Bay–Shore Greenbelt...Brooklyn Mini-Runs
...Bay Ridge–Gravesend Bay–Shore
Parkway...Brooklyn Mini-Runs

QUEENS Flushing Meadow Park...Alley Park...   62
Rockaway Beach...Kissena Park and
Corridor Park...Forest Park...
Cunningham Park... Queens Mini-Runs

BRONX Van Cortlandt Park...Van Cortlandt Park–   83
Croton Aqueduct...Pelham Bay Park...
New York Botanical Garden...Riverdale–
Palisade Avenue...Bronx River Parkway
...Bronx Mini-Runs

STATEN Clove Lakes Park...Silver Lake...   102
ISLAND Great Kills Park...South Beach–
Oakwood Beach ...Staten Island Mini-Runs

LONG RUNS Manhattan...Brooklyn...Queens...Bronx 114
...Staten Island...Palisades Interstate
Park–George Washington Bridge...
Thursday Night Bridge Run...
Old Croton Aqueduct

METROPOLITAN AREA RUNNING CLUBS   119

ANNUAL ROAD RACES   122

RUNNING TRACKS   124

INDOOR RUNNING TRACKS   125

NEW YORK CITY RUNNING RULES   126

FOREWORD

In January of 1978, two recent converts to long-distance running, Patti Hagan and Joe Cody, walked into my office with a good idea. They proposed to inventory all the running areas in New York City. It was something I had had in mind myself for quite a while. I encouraged them and assured them of the full support of the New York Road Runners Club. I provided the names of prominent city runners for them to contact, mentioning Joe Kleinerman, Ted Corbitt, and Dr. Norb Sander, among others. They set out with high enthusiasm.

A year and a half later, Patti and Joe have completed their long-distance legwork. They have run and measured all the routes they describe, often in different seasons. As New York Road Runners Club members they have participated in races in all the boroughs, from summer speed runs to the New York City Marathon. They have spoken to most of the leading runners and running officials in New York City. They have thoroughly covered the New York running scene.

I am both proud and pleased to give the New York Road Runners Club's endorsement and support to an effort that will remain the standard reference for running in New York City for many years.

Fred Lebow
President,
New York Road Runners Club

INTRODUCTION

New York is quite possibly the most-run city in America. It is large and has many parks, as well as a populace tolerant of and even friendly to runners. The two men who have had the biggest influence on New York running had nothing to do with running.

In the nineteenth century, Frederick Law Olmsted (with Calvert Vaux) designed America's first great urban park, Central Park, now the core of New York running. He followed Central with Prospect Park and Fort Greene Park, in Brooklyn, and with Riverside Park, Morningside Park, and the original idea for Inwood Hill Park, in Manhattan. (His son, Frederick Law Olmsted, Jr., landscaped Fort Tryon Park.) A century later, all these, except Morningside, are runners' parks. In the twentieth century, Moses—Robert Moses—did the rest. From the mind of Moses, Chairman of the Triborough Bridge and Tunnel Authority, the following places came either whole, or transformed to his inspiration: Pelham Bay Park, Bronx Park, Mosholu Parkway, and Van Cortlandt Park, in the Bronx; Randall's and Ward's Islands; East River Park, in Manhattan; the Belt Parkway, Coney Island, and Marine Park, in Brooklyn; Clove Lakes and Silver Lake Parks, South Beach, Great Kills Park, and Willowbrook Park, on Staten Island; Flushing Meadow Park, Kissena Park, Kissena Corridor Park, Cunningham Park, Alley Park, Rockaway Park, Jacob Riis Park, Astoria Park, Forest Park, Highland Park, and Baisley Pond Park, in Queens; and many of the bridge links between the boroughs. Moses created "parkways" for cars and, to get the financing for them, threw in coordinate parks for people. Recently, runners have discovered his routes and have reclaimed some areas for pedestrians. Between them, Olmsted and Moses are responsible for all but five of the runs mapped in this book. Olmsted and Moses put New York City on the running map and shaped the New York City runner's landscape more profoundly than any runner ever has.

In the 1970's, New York City became the capital of the known running world, with its own enterprising and benevolent czar, Fred Lebow. In 1976, his New York Road Runners Club moved the New York City Marathon, until then a circular race, out of Central Park and linked the five boroughs in an ingeniously designed 26.2-mile linear race. People along the route became aware of road-running, the simplicity of its basic two-step. The marathon field expanded from a hundred and twenty-six runners in 1970 to fourteen thousand in 1979. Instead of a few old-timers scrounging up a race every so often, races were *organized*, every weekend, throughout the city, often with corporate backing and T-shirts. Running clinics drew hundreds. If you didn't run, what did you do?

As soon became evident, there were as many ways to run New York as there were New York runners. By the late seventies, it was hard to find a place, or an hour, where the runner was not. The runner was a new kind of urban athlete. Where basketball had been the street game, running became the street sport. Everyone could join in and everyone did. Running was the first mass fitness movement to take New York City, which had been known as a town of raucous sports fans. Running had the potential to open up the whole city. Borough provincials began to see the connections between Manhattan and Brooklyn and Queens and the Bronx, and even Staten Island, at least on Marathon Day. New York runners were not fussy. They would run on any surface—asphalt, dirt, grass, concrete, cinder. Runners were like weeds on the move, everywhere. Some parks got so crowded that runners began tripping over one another. The only questions around town were "Do you run?" and "Where?" Runners talked routes, only to discover that most of their routes, most of the time, were concentrated in a few obvious, and overrun, places: Central Park, Riverside Park, the East River Jogging Path, Clove Lakes Park, Prospect Park, Flushing Meadow Park, and Van Cortlandt Park.

It turned out that many people were one-park runners. And after several years of running one park, they were getting bored with the repetition. Some stuck to one part of one park, like the Central Park Reservoir runners. Some ran in a fast pack almost oblivious to their surroundings, like the Thursday night Bridge Runners (Central Park to the George Washington). Marathoners became bored, getting in their weekly Long Run by looping the same loop ad infinitum. Addicts figured out how to run to work, then realized that there was no shower at the office. Many New York distance sticklers wanted to get off the beaten path, but did not know the exact distance elsewhere. Most New Yorkers keep track; miles-per-week must be recorded, faithfully, in the runner's diary. Many city runners were hesitant to free-lance new routes through foreign neighborhoods.

Diligent runners eventually reach the stage at which they begin to judge the world in terms of good places to run. They notice that in the city you can always find something to run around, even if it's only the square block you live on, and the measure is ready-made at twenty city blocks to the mile. They discover that New York has more soft spots and green spots than seems possible—greenery in parks and on belts jumps off the maps. They begin to consider cemetery perimeters, reservoir rims, apartment complexes such as Stuyvesant Town, and small islands like Roosevelt and Ward's and Randall's. They discover that it's more interesting to run from one place to some other place, instead of always running in circles. They try to follow a street beyond the known turf and they find they don't fall off the edge of the city. East Side runners have traditionally been reluctant to go beyond the end of the East River Jogging Path, 3.25 miles along the Upper East River. There was a missing link, but few runners ventured north to find it.

The fun of running New York, as runners are learning, is that almost any place can be run and the links are good. Running provides an enjoyable way of exploring the city. It's the chance to understand the city in your bones, and if your cruising speed is around nine minutes a mile, that's slow enough to notice the changes, the shadings from one neighborhood to the next. The fun of exploration *à pied*, the satisfaction of extending your concrete knowledge of your surroundings, is self-reinforcing. It makes you want to do it again, to expand the range of your foot wanderings. It's possible to make route design a minor hobby and to choreograph a Long Run for every borough. There's a lot of satisfaction in knowing the city turf cold. Running gives easy lessons in urban geography, sociology, anthropology—makes you see with your feet how things fit together here. In Lower Manhattan and under the Brooklyn Bridge, you can run past spice warehouses where you smell the cinnamon and curry fresh off the boat. Runs take you past bakeries and bread factories (as happens in Flushing Meadow Park, Prospect Park, and Van Cortlandt Park), and the fragrance is enough to keep you circling, breathing deeply. You develop a new kind of memory for the city. You begin to remember it by smells, by hills, by seasons, by potholes, by feel as well as by sight. Having run the Brooklyn Bridge is a lot more memorable than simply having seen it. Having drunk from the mineral spring in Pelham Bay Park, is there any need to continue importing Perrier? And everything seems, ultimately, to refer back to Manhattan. The Manhattan skyline keeps following you, popping up when you thought you were farthest from it. Running changes the proportions and the relationships between things. Depending on the distance you are willing to run, you can, from the Rockaways or Riverdale, reduce Manhattan to the size of a nailhead.

New York City has indeed become *the* place to run in the United States. There are special pleasures here: the classic skyline, the friendly natives, the superlative city parks of America, the abundance of fellow runners, a great people's marathon. In short, running is the year-round New York sport that is wonderfully cheap (until you get injured); there is no country club to join, no place where running *must* be done, no equipment beyond comfortable shoes. The runner develops a special appreciation of the city in knowing the footing, the foliage, the architecture in minute detail, the keen sense of having New York in the arch of your foot.

New York City has everything for the runner. In New York, you can run boardwalks—at Coney Island, in the Rockaways, on the Brooklyn Bridge. You can run beaches—South Beach, Great Kills Beach, Orchard Beach. You can run great parks—Central, Prospect, Van Cortlandt, Pelham Bay. You can run skyscrapers—the Empire State once a year and others by special dispensation. You can run tracks, both indoor and out. You can run bridges—the Triborough, the George Washington, the Williamsburg, among others. You can run rivers—the Hudson, the East, the Harlem, the Bronx. You can run in the streets, on the sidewalks, beside the parkways; you can run circles, squares, triangles, rectangles, trapezoids, rhomboids, hexagons—up buildings or around them, with orthotics or without. New York is like Alice's Restaurant: You can run any way you want. The trails are there (the hole in the fence always comes just when you need it). Here are directions for finding them.

10

HOW TO USE THE ROAD RUNNER'S GUIDE

City runners usually have to plan their runs, depending on the time of day or year. The Road Runner's Guide to New York City is offered as a complete handbook to the most interesting, challenging, scenic, relaxing, historical, refreshing, unpolluted city runs of from a third of a mile to 44 miles, in Manhattan, Brooklyn, Queens, the Bronx, and Staten Island—with the links between them. There is a map of the New York City Marathon route and a detailed course description. The book includes thirty maps accompanying turn-by-turn course descriptions of major runs, as well as notes for short, simple runs, called Mini-Runs, in places like Washington Square Park in the Village, the third-of-a-mile Brooklyn Heights Promenade, the Jerome Park Reservoir in the Bronx—small places that people do run, of which they might want the correct measure and some picture.

The guide is organized by borough. Each chapter is introduced by a borough map that shows, at a glance, the major running areas therein and the mileage of the connecting runs between, from which we have designed a Long Run for each borough: Manhattan Long Run, 31 miles; Brooklyn Long Run, 44 miles (27.6 miles abbreviated); Queens Long Run, 20 miles; the Bronx Long Run, 24.5 miles; and the Staten Island Long Run, 22.5 miles.

We have given a character sketch of each major run and technical information under the headings:

1. **FOOTING** (terrain, surface, conditions)
2. **COURSE DIRECTIONS** (detailed, turn right, turn left)
3. **OTHER RUNS** (within the mapped area, such as cinder tracks)
4. **HAZARDS** (what to watch out for)
5. **COMFORTS** (water, restrooms)
6. **MASS TRANSPORT** (subway and bus information, parking)
7. **EXTENSIONS** (connecting runs to other areas)

An alphabet box gives the length of the mapped course legs, so that by simple addition of legs you can design your own routes with a precise distance in mind. For example, the Riverside Drive (pg. 28) segments (in miles) between Seventy-second Street and the George Washington Bridge are A = 1.2 miles, B = 1.30, C = 1.80, D = 1.15. A + B + C + D = 5.5 miles. Measurements are exact to the nearest tenth of a mile. (1 mile = 1.61 kilometers; .62 mile = 1 kilometer; 1 yard = .9144 meter; 1.0936 yard = 1 meter.)

Early on, we discovered that the least accurate way to find out the length of a course is to ask another runner. Runners tend to be generous with themselves. A ten per cent standard deductible should be taken off any estimate another runner gives you. Every route listed in the guide has been run and measured by the authors, who interviewed regular runners of the route for particulars and when possible ran the distance with them.

Patti Hagan, Joe Cody
New York City
July 1979

THE NEW YORK CITY MARATHON

Since few of the tens of thousands of feet starting in the New York City Marathon ever have a chance to pre tread the course, this block-by-pothole profile of the 26.2 miles run the third Sunday in October may be of strategic help, especially for those who plan on running and seeing.

The New York course offers almost as much to the eye as to the lungs and legs—a visually rich tour-de-foot of New York's neighborhood villages, architecture, history, and peoples. The harbor view from the Verrazano-Narrows Bridge starting point puts Manhattan in perspective—a compact, scaled-down, remote version that is only a part of a much larger New York. Yet the Manhattan that all roads lead to remains a reference point throughout the run. Isolated Manhattan skymarks—the World Trade Center, the Empire State Building, the Chrysler Building, Citicorp Center—are glimpsed again and again during the first thirteen miles, like stray pieces of a landscape puzzle. From the Pulaski Bridge, the pieces, in profile, define a skyline only slightly less splendid than the cityscape viewed from the crest of the Queensboro Bridge.

The city's size and scale change en route from the wide-open row-house flats of Brooklyn and Queens to the sky-obliterating scrapers of Manhattan. The skyscrapers and clock towers, especially the clock tower of the Williamsburgh Savings Bank, Brooklyn's skyscraper, give the runner long-lasting durable eyeholds, visual pulleys that mark progress as they grow and diminish in size.

As to the road itself—if no road can be said to be perfect, any New York City road can be said to be less perfect than almost all others. The New York City Marathon may offer few hills, but there is challenge enough in the pavement. Consider the pothole. By March, each year, the city Transportation Department has filled upward of a quarter of a million potholes caused by winter but calculates that another million and a half remain, of which we mention only the most significant. Look for them toward the curb edges of roads, at major intersections, and on the lips of manhole covers. In many places, the road has a crackled ceramic texture; in others, antique trolley tracks have surfaced through the asphalt. Elsewhere are cobblestones. Keep at least one eye to the road, for pitfalls and potholes abound. Roads in Brooklyn and Queens tend to be turtlebacked—flattest at road center, with the greatest curvature toward the edge. Those in Manhattan and the Bronx tend to be swaybacked. New York City roads suffer the same injury syndromes as New York City runners—these roads pronate, these roads have shin splints, these roads have stress fractures, and possibly even chondromalacia.

Verrazano–Narrows Bridge

Starter's howitzer goes off ten-thirty sharp. Pick up the Blue Line. First mile upbridge, concrete road, Masonite-covered expansion joints. Upgrade scarcely noticed because of exalted harbor views—minimalist Manhattan to left, Europe to right. Run-guru advice, "Listen to your body," worthless.

Listen to your brain, go slowly, take in the astonishing view, the swarm of helicopters. Marathoners' feet the only feet ever allowed on Verrazano. (Verrazano—first European to see this area, 1524; his eponymous bridge, 1964.) First sighting of Williamsburgh Savings Bank clock tower, eight-mile point, to left. A landmark worth holding on to. Mile 2, downbridge, to Brooklyn.

Women and rookie male marathoners start on left side, top level, Verrazano, exit left, dip and climb to Ninety-second Street, left again on Fort Hamilton Parkway, down to Ninety-fourth, right up to Fourth Avenue, and right again. These runners also get an extra water station, at the end of the bridge, before merging with the other runners. Experienced marathon men start on top level, right side of bridge, exit right funneling down a narrow, steep ramp onto Dahlgren Place, up to Ninety-second and left across road to two far-right lanes. Notice stern Nordic stone masks over doorjambs of three brick row houses on right after Fort Hamilton Parkway.

Bay Ridge

Possibility of a runner-jam at Ninety-second and Fourth Avenue convergence. Fourth Avenue, for New York, is a tolerably well-paved, well-maintained road, despite a pronounced crown. Best keep to center road. Intersections, as in all segments of the course, tend to be fairly choppy with occasional clusters of rimmed manhole covers. Five-mile stretch of Fourth Avenue generally flat, with mild rises and downgrades. Fourth Avenue, beginning in Scandinavian-Italian Bay Ridge, passes through a series of old ethnic neighborhoods. Many retain the marks (and churches) of previous inhabitants.

Three-mile mark, Eighty-fourth Street, water station. Expect water oases each mile for duration of run. Tidy churches, steeples, gardens along this portion. Exposed trolley tracks at Bay Ridge Avenue.

Sunset Park

Once Finnish, now Hispanic. At Sixty-fifth, stay to right of divider. In Forties blocks, look left for views of New York Harbor. Hope for a sea breeze. Williamsburgh clock tower again visible at Forty-fifth Street, five-mile point and first E.R.G. station. (Be glad you practiced runnin' n' drinkin'.) Check your time on the digital clock. E.R.G. and clocks will be repeated at five-mile intervals.

Fortieth Street, tread carefully, potpourri of potholes at midroad. Twenty-eighth Street, World Trade Center on left. Twenty-seventh Street, right, St. Rocco Youth Center—wonder how many times this year spectators will favor runners with theme song from *Rocky*—runner's schmaltz—over speakers hanging out windows. Twenty-sixth Street, center lane, four-inch-square gas hole without lid, good for at least a sprained ankle. Stay left. Twenties, left, junkies nodding out on funeral-parlor steps.

Gowanus–Park Slope

After Prospect Avenue, Gowanus to left, Park Slope to right. Gowanus named for Mohawk Indian chief Gowane; scene of fierce fighting during Battle of Long Island, George Washington's first engagement of the Revolution. Many Americans lost their lives here, some drowning during retreat across the Gowanus Creek. Now an Italian stronghold.

Park Slope ascends gradually to Prospect Park, an area of born-again brownstones and brownstoners. By Tenth Street, gaining noticeably on Williamsburgh clock tower. Sixth to Bergen, da Brooklyn Flats, a somewhat monotonous and depressed area. Dead ahead, now almost life-sized, the clock tower. At Degraw Street, center and left lanes, three large raised steel plates, good for a trip-up.

Crossing at Flatbush Avenue, appropriately flat. Breeze around base of clock tower and the 1908 Brooklyn Academy of Music. Enrico Caruso sang here. Good place to station a friend, remember to run on friend's side of street. Dead ahead on Ashland Place, see upper stories of Art Deco Chrysler Building, Forty-second Street, Manhattan!

Fort Greene–Clinton Hill

Some of the most interesting old New York architecture stands along the Lafayette Avenue stretch—brownstone mansions, New England-style clapboard houses, Gothic churches, Tiffany church windows, Victorian brick row houses. Enough intact stoops here for "No Loitering or Sitting on Stoop" signs. Alas, roadway not equal to scenery—trolley tracks cum potholes, exposed cobblestones, urban frost heaves, and gouges from snowplow blades. Cross-country training excellent preparation for Lafayette Avenue, a ragged, ragged road.

Left down South Elliott Place, Fort Greene Park, with remains of ten thousand Americans who perished in British prisoner-of-war ships anchored in Wallabout Bay during the Revolution. (Pass Wallabout Street later.)

For carbohydrate unloading, Port-O-Sans will be stationed behind the fence of the Bishop Laughlin High School track at Clermont Avenue, right. Surface of Lafayette undulates feverishly, gradually uptending. Look up for stone hallows of Our Lady Queen of All Saints Church while scouting hollows in the road.

Some runners will be too late for Sunday-morning gospel singing at the Apostolic Faith Mission, Washington and Lafayette. Surface improves at St. James Street, passing Pratt Institute, a technical school founded in 1887 by Brooklyn oil baron Charles Pratt.

Bedford–Stuyvesant

Largest black community in New York. From Classon Avenue to Bedford Avenue road deteriorates to a disaster, with an everlasting work-in-progress mess at the corner of Bedford and Lafayette—unfilled holes and raised steel plates. Cut a sharp left at the corner, then hold to the middle.

Disco, *salsa*, soul, rock, and gospel music shared with the street. Expect encouragement, especially from neighborhood kids who'll identify your brand of sneakers (if possible), comment on your T-shirt, slap five, and ask, "Why you be runnin', anyway?" Medieval road conditions, a plague of potholes.

Straight ahead, sheared angle-topped Citicorp Center. On a hot day hoses at the ready at Engine Company 209, where twin towers of World Trade Center come into view on left. Park Avenue (another Park Avenue) and Bedford, a real washboard of an intersection; at ten-mile E.R.G. point (Flushing Avenue and Bedford), four trolley rails, exposed cobblestones, mess of manhole lids—savage footing. Plant feet carefully. Some depressions at Wallabout Street.

Williamsburg

Hasidic-Hispanic area. At Rutledge Street, to right, faces on some pediments stonily examine runners, as do groups of bearded Hasidic Jews dressed in black coats, fur hats. Male-dominated community out of eighteenth-century Europe. Rare Victorian mansions along Bedford Avenue. Passing over Brooklyn–Queens Expressway, look back over left shoulder for a diminished Williamsburgh clock tower. Bumpy road over flat terrain, but Lafayette was worse. Williamsburg the setting for Betty Smith's novel *A Tree Grows in Brooklyn*. The ailanthus—tenement palm to some—still grows here.

Around South Eighth Street neighborhood relaxes considerably, shading from Hasidic to Hispanic, and audience support picks up. At Broadway, judge which way the wind blows from weathervane atop dome of Williamsburgh Savings Bank's mother bank. Enjoy views of exquisite United Mutual Savings Bank, East River, Williamsburg Bridge.

Greenpoint

Good road from Williamsburg Bridge to Greenpoint, mainly downtending and flat. Cross into Greenpoint at McCarren Park. Nice view of Manhattan skyline on left, five onion domes of Russian Orthodox Cathedral of the Transfiguration on right. Bedford Avenue, last block, uptending. Acned road surface, pocked with closely laid manhole covers, ancient trolley tracks, and tar calluses and bunions.

Manhattan Avenue, Greenpoint's main street, flat with a slight rise to St. Anthony of Padua Church on right—check your elapsed time on church clock tower. Stay to mid-road. Old brick buildings along Manhattan Avenue frame Citicorp Center, forming a twentieth-century abstract architecture. Greenpoint, home to Poles, Germans, Ukrainians, calls to mind a European village with its tidy shops and people, including second-story window watchers resting on pillows. Alleged birthplace of Brooklynese. Actual birthplace of Mae West. Greenpointers, enthusiastic marathon watchers, call out your number or T-shirt logo.

Just past St. Anthony's, a downgrade begins, perceptible only to feet, until you turn corner onto Greenpoint Avenue—three downhill blocks to build momentum, do some inadvertent fartlek before half-marathon mark.

THE NEW YORK CITY MARATHON

A 26.2 mile ethnic tour through urban villages

Map by George Colbert and Guenter Vollath
Map captions by Patti Hagan and Joe Cody

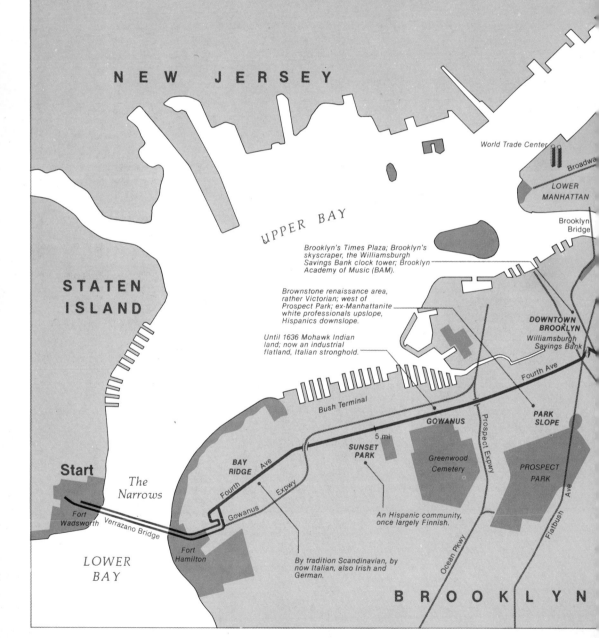

NEW JERSEY

STATEN ISLAND

UPPER BAY

World Trade Center

Broadway

LOWER MANHATTAN

Brooklyn Bridge

Brooklyn's Times Plaza; Brooklyn's skyscraper, the Williamsburgh Savings Bank clock tower; Brooklyn Academy of Music (BAM).

Brownstone renaissance area, rather Victorian; west of Prospect Park; ex-Manhattanite white professionals upslope, Hispanics downslope.

Until 1636 Mohawk Indian land; now an industrial flatland, Italian stronghold.

DOWNTOWN BROOKLYN

Williamsburgh Savings Bank

Fourth Ave

Bush Terminal

GOWANUS

PARK SLOPE

5 mi

SUNSET PARK

Greenwood Cemetery

Prospect Expwy

PROSPECT PARK

Start

The Narrows

BAY RIDGE

Fourth Ave

Gowanus Expwy

Fort Wadsworth

Verrazano Bridge

Fort Hamilton

Gowanus

An Hispanic community, once largely Finnish.

Ocean Pkwy

Flatbush Ave

LOWER BAY

By tradition Scandinavian, by now Italian, also Irish and German.

BROOKLYN

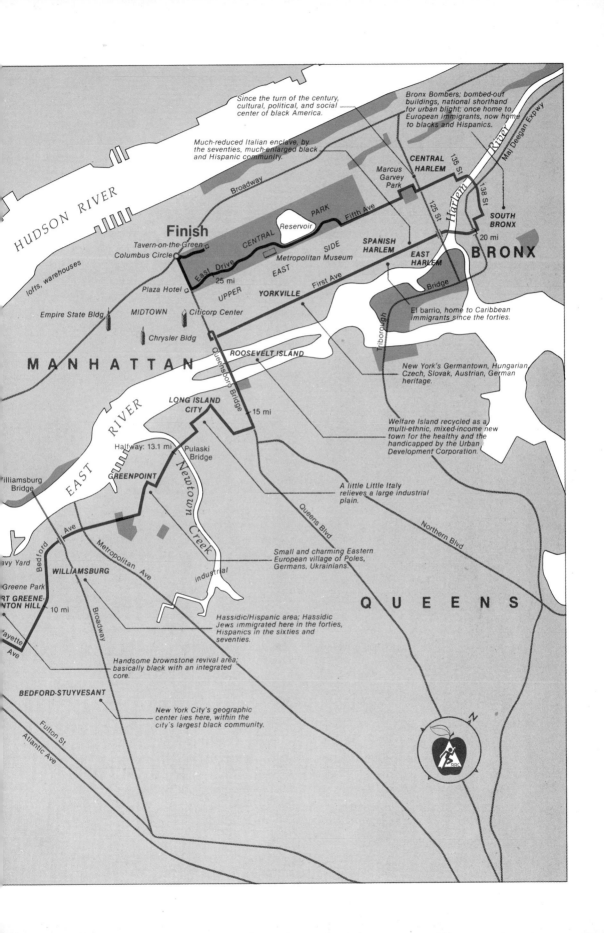

HUDSON RIVER

lofts, warehouses

Since the turn of the century, cultural, political, and social center of black America.

Much-reduced Italian enclave, by the seventies, much-enlarged black and Hispanic community.

Bronx Bombers; bombed-out buildings, national shorthand for urban blight; once home to European immigrants, now home to blacks and Hispanics.

Maj Deegan Expwy

Harlem River

Broadway

CENTRAL HARLEM

135 St

138 St

Marcus Garvey Park

125 St

SOUTH BRONX

Finish

Tavern-on-the-Green

Columbus Circle

Reservoir

CENTRAL PARK

Fifth Ave

SPANISH HARLEM

EAST HARLEM

BRONX

20 mi

Plaza Hotel

Metropolitan Museum

East Drive

25 mi

EAST SIDE

UPPER

YORKVILLE

First Ave

Bridge

El barrio, home to Caribbean immigrants since the forties.

Empire State Bldg

MIDTOWN

Citicorp Center

Chrysler Bldg

M A N H A T T A N

Queensboro Bridge

ROOSEVELT ISLAND

Tiborough

New York's Germantown, Hungarian, Czech, Slovak, Austrian, German heritage.

LONG ISLAND CITY

15 mi

Welfare Island recycled as a multi-ethnic, mixed-income new town for the healthy and the handicapped by the Urban Development Corporation.

EAST

RIVER

Halfway: 13.1 mi

Pulaski Bridge

Newtown Creek

A little Little Italy relieves a large industrial plain.

Queens Blvd

Northern Blvd

'illiamsburg Bridge

GREENPOINT

Bedford Ave

Metropolitan Ave

industrial

Small and charming Eastern European village of Poles, Germans, Ukrainians.

avy Yard

WILLIAMSBURG

Q U E E N S

Greene Park

RT GREENE-NTON HILL

10 mi

Broadway

ayette Ave

Hassidic/Hispanic area; Hassidic Jews immigrated here in the forties, Hispanics in the sixties and seventies.

Handsome brownstone revival area; basically black with an integrated core.

BEDFORD-STUYVESANT

Fulton St

Atlantic Ave

New York City's geographic center lies here, within the city's largest black community.

N

RRC

At Pulaski Bridge (named for Polish nobleman who came to America to aid patriots) over Newtown Creek, a choice—to run on concrete sidewalk, narrow and likely to be crowded, or to take bridge roadway with raised steel plates, five irregular expansion joints on each side, and a long, studded grating that makes for an ankle-wrenching crossing. Slow down, run flat-footed. Don't try to pass. Extremely hazardous.

Queens

Roadway through Queens exceptionally flat. Check time on steeple of St. Mary's church, Forty-ninth Avenue and Vernon Boulevard, while running toward the Empire State Building and the Chrysler Building. Newly paved surface on Vernon. Runner passes over small railroad bridge and through a little Little Italy. Don't worry that you might be running backward when you run past a street you think you just ran past. By some bizarre rule of Queens street nomenclature, Forty-seventh Avenue follows Forty-seventh Road, Forty-sixth Avenue follows Forty-sixth Road, etc.

Stay to middle of Forty-fourth Drive, a bleak, light-industry drag. Rough pock-holed road, slightly upclined, from Forty-fourth Drive to Queensboro (Fifty-ninth Street) Bridge approach. Though neither the steepest nor the longest climb of the race, coming at the fifteen-mile mark, the Queensboro is the New York Marathon's Heartbreak Hill. The runners' lane is narrow— three runners wide. Runners can choose to cross on bridge grating, relatively smooth and comfortable to the feet, or on a three-feet-wide carpet, which some say is too soft.

Upper East Side and Yorkville

Port-O-Sans tucked into vest-pocket park on Fifty-ninth Street, beneath bridge. Hairpin left turn down ramp from bridge to First Avenue. Runners dropped into natural amphitheater. Large, lusty crowds here boost runners with a contact high that banishes any idea of an early-Manhattan dropout.

Stay to left of divider beginning at Eighty-first Street. Generally uphill from Fifty-ninth Street Bridge to Eighty-fifth; a series of downhill steps through Yorkville. You can look good in Yorkville! Downgrade continues through the Nineties. From Eightieth to Eighty-fifth, First Avenue is a sight—a mosaic of tar patches, waffled surfaces, ruts, and potholed manhole covers.

Spanish and East Harlem

Cheers of the First Avenue crowd will be ringing in your ears as you continue north, the Bronx clearly in sight. Crowds thinner through *El Barrio*, tenements of Fiorello La Guardia's home turf, and upper East Harlem projects. A few craters at 111th Street, to Willis Avenue Bridge.

Runners can choose bridge sidewalk or roadway. Expansion joints on gradual upgrade nothing serious, just be aware of them. On downhill side, over-expanded expansion joints. Studded grating midbridge will tear at your feet. Careful. Randall's Island to right, extinct community of Mott

Haven—now part of the South Bronx—straight ahead as you cross Harlem River. One horrendous expansion joint at top of descent ramp.

South Bronx

Last set of Port-O-Sans, on 135th Street, on right side, after leaving Willis Avenue Bridge. The wall, the twenty-mile mark, can usually be met at the far end of the Willis Avenue Bridge. Fortunately, the wall is followed by a long, smooth downhill block. Step lively over 1879 sewer covers as you turn onto Alexander Avenue.

Stay toward double yellow center stripe on 138th, considering the mine-field of potholes, exposed cobbles, and trolley tracks. Pass two famous New York streets, Park Avenue (the fancy one) and the Grand Concourse. Uphill from Park Avenue to Madison Avenue Bridge. Take care on making the step up onto the notorious foot-high curb of the sidewalk route. Many runners find this step of Himalayan size. Marathoners may be able to cross on bridge roadway, with only the studded grating to worry about. No troublesome expansion joints.

Harlem

Long gradual downhill run off Madison Avenue Bridge and a right turn onto 135th Street followed by a left onto Fifth Avenue. See Empire State Building from corner of 135th and Fifth. Perhaps inspiring? Don't be faked out by the trees dead ahead. They're in Marcus Garvey park, not Central Park. Street here is disintegrating, as is much of the housing. Enthusiastic crowds: Some elders say, "God bless you." Kids love to slap five, play the running-shoes-name game.

Route goes right, around Marcus Garvey Park (formerly Mount Morris Park), and down Fifth Avenue from 120th. Surface fraught with gouges and bumps in low and high relief. Pass blocks of burned-out, dead-eyed tenements. Flat until upgrade, 107th to 102nd.

Central Park

Home to many runners, especially New York Road Runners Club. Almost there, only three miles to go. Good running surface, some gentle hills that may seem mountainous. Follow the Blue Line. Yellow and white circles mark all pockholes and imperfections. You must leave the security of the park at Fifty-ninth Street, the Plaza, for three long, slightly uphill blocks. Reenter park at Columbus Circle, the finish line for the first American marathon in 1896 (Stamford, Connecticut, to New York approximately thirty-five miles on the roads). Cut left across a triangle of grass and pick up the West Drive. Slight uphill push to finish line outside Tavern-on-the-Green. Observe digital clock for your own time, because volunteers at the three finish chutes won't be concerned with times. They'll be too busy ripping the bar code off your number so the race results can be tabulated by the computer.

Sheep Meadow! Friends! Medics! Drinks! End of the long Blue Line.

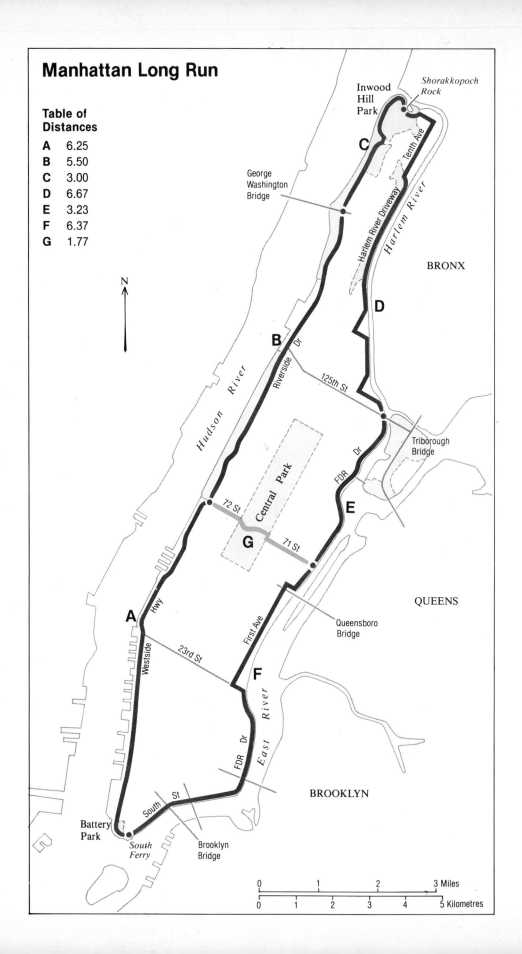

Manhattan Long Run

**Table of
Distances**

A	6.25
B	5.50
C	3.00
D	6.67
E	3.23
F	6.37
G	1.77

N

Shorakkopoch Rock

Inwood Hill Park

C

Tenth Ave

George Washington Bridge

Harlem River Driveway

Harlem River

BRONX

B

Riverside Dr

125th St

D

Hudson River

Dr

FDR

Triborough Bridge

Central Park

72 St

G

71 St

E

QUEENS

A

Hwy

First Ave

23rd St

Westside

F

Queensboro Bridge

FDR Dr

East River

BROOKLYN

South St

Battery Park

South Ferry

Brooklyn Bridge

0		1		2		3 Miles

0	1	2	3	4	5 Kilometres

MANHATTAN

Manhattan is a runner's magnet. More races are held in Manhattan than in any other borough, and more people come to Manhattan specifically to run. To run Manhattan is to run the core of the Big Apple: Central Park, spiritual home to New York runners. Everyone eventually shows up in Central Park for a race—as many as four thousand for a mid-week, midsummer night's 3.5-mile race.

Manhattan's running preeminence has to do with the New York Road Runners Club, which sits on the western sidelines of Central Park. Because of the N.Y.R.R.C., Manhattan presents the extreme of organized running—Central Park running clinics every Saturday, frequent mid-week lecture clinics, races most weekends—under Fred Lebow, New York running's energetic godfather. Lebow can as often be found near the finish line of a N.Y.R.R.C. race with a broom in his hand, tidying up the grounds, as running the streets of Manhattan. He is not just an evangelist of running as a sport but a proponent of running-to-everything, having spent the month of February 1979, running to work, to appointments, to social engagements. He logged 238 miles. Lebow has *made* running in New York City, and made his organization into if not one of the city's powers, one of its most visible principalities.

Manhattan, of all the boroughs, lends itself most easily to foot. And the all-but A.A.U.-certified 31-mile route for footing the Manhattan perimeter was pieced together in 1955 by Ted Corbitt, New York's patron ultra-marathoner and Olympian. In that year Corbitt moved to Marble Hill on the Bronx border, and began running the 11.6 miles to and from work downtown. Corbitt's Manhattan Long Run keeps to the island's coastline and provides the best overall look at Manhattan's runners and running habitats.

Being able to run Manhattan's boundary seems to reduce a city that often feels too big, to a comprehensible, even friendly, size. On the Long Run, Manhattan's profile stretches out beside you, punctuated by many familiar shapes. The runner passes by an architect's lineup—every style of the past hundred years side-by-side—Manhattan mug shots.

Even though Manhattan's most challenging runs lie at its northern extreme, in the wilderness of Inwood Hill Park (a running spot since the thirties), most Manhattan runners stick to the crowded paths of Central Park, Riverside Park, or the East River. And in mid-Manhattan it's almost hard to find a place or an hour that's free of runners.

But the grand finale, after you have run Manhattan's various parks, is to pick up Ted Corbitt's run. Until recently, Corbitt was one of the few runners to do his loop regularly, four hours ten minutes on the average for the thirty-one miles, though once he did it in 3:42 "in street shoes." Having once strung Manhattan together, Corbitt had in fact designed an ultra-marathoner's dream loop. While training for a 100-mile or a twenty-four hour race, he has often looped Manhattan twice on the same day, even twice on each of three consecutive days of the Labor Day weekend, to celebrate. Corbitt's average time for two times around is nine or ten hours, though once, "in a high state," he ran it in eight. So, if you want 62, do Manhattan twice. If you want less, catch the subway home.

CENTRAL PARK

6-mile loop

Central Park is doubtless the most heavily overrun 6-mile course in the United States, and quite possibly in the world. Only a few years back, in Central Park as elsewhere, running was the most resisted of participant sports, while softball and tennis were the big draws. Now, Manhattan's eight-hundred-and-forty-acre central green has become the city-runner's common. Runner traffic in Central Park is not yet so heavy as to warrant one-way running, but it does have the look of a mass movement, especially on weekends when the crowding causes tangles between bikers, runners, and skaters. Central Park is the place to feel that you're running on a trendmill, and to remark, how widespread is the species *Runner*, how various are its getups.

Central Park has become, over the past few years, a prime runner habitat. Runner watching gets to be like bird watching (there is much of both in Central Park); keep in mind the standard traits and field markings: stripes, dots, dashes, swooshes (on shoes and shorts); coloration (black on orange, white on blue, yellow on red); souvenir T-shirts (Boston, Yonkers, New York, Jersey Shore); peculiarities of gait (high knee action, sensuous supination, a certain hand-flop; it's a little harder to tell who's wearing orthotics or powder puffs for heel lifts); and response upon sighting. Some rate Central Park the least friendly running place in New York City. Even run regulars, those runners on your same time and training schedule, don't usually smile or say hello. In fact, certain runners seem to pronate hostility.

Frederick Law Olmsted and Calvert Vaux laid out their Greensward—Central Park—on paper in 1858. Fred Lebow, New York's running impresario, laid out his first Central Park New York City Marathon course in 1970. By October 1858 Olmsted and Vaux were planting trees—thousands—by hand, in Central Park. By October 1978, Lebow was timing, electronically and by hand, the 8,588 finishers of the five-borough New York City Marathon as they collapsed in the Central Park Sheep Meadow. The Park is a National Historic Landmark as well as being the city's first designated Scenic Landmark, and though most runners, deep in their aerobic highs or lows, steaming through another weekend race, may not realize it, when running Central Park they are running one of America's great works of art. The steady nine-minute miler can complete the classic six-mile work in fifty-four minutes, and the daily Central Park habitué can fix its particulars in mind by repetition.

For instance, a pause while heading south, at Balcony Bridge (opposite West Seventy-seventh Street) overlooking The Lake, gives one of the great skyline views of Manhattan floating above trees, with the exquisite cast-iron Bow Bridge in the foreground. Across The Lake stands The Ramble, the Park's most thickly wooded and most heavily birded portion. The Park Drive passes over a dozen ornamental-functional bridges, and by a lot of statuary. To date, however, runners have not monumentalized themselves. In fact, the thousands who daily circle the park have left no reminder save the Marathon Blue Line that enters the park at East 102nd. (The daily encounter with Mile 24 of the New York City Marathon, painted in a kind of Morse code, can pique your marathon hopes through the worst of shin splints.)

In a sense, runners have made vehicular history in Central Park. Between 1899, when the first automobiles were allowed on the Park Drive, and 1962 when the first race was held on the park's roads(a 25kmMilk Run)the automobile ruled the park, although the roads had been designed specifically to make speeding difficult. Olmsted and Vaux threw a lot of curves. Moreover, during the past few years, with the generous help of the city's Department of Parks and Recreation, footpower has gained the strength to drive the cars out of the park by the days-per-year—weekends from 7 P.M. Friday to 6 A.M. Monday, and for eight hours of every weekday, May 1 through October 31. With the banishment of cars has come an exotic commingling of traffic on the Park Drive—skaters, cyclists, runners, skate-skiers, skateboarders, horse carriages. This might well have astounded Olmsted and Vaux, who carefully designed paths with bridges for traffic separation in order to segregate and make safe each class of traffic from every other.

Central Park has enough hills to be rated a tough course, hills shaped about seventy-five thousand years ago, when the Wisconsin ice sheet scraped by. But despite such topography, Central Park remains the chic place to run among those who care about running and being seen. There are plenty of type-A, intense chronograph-fixated runners training here, getting in their speed work through the northern hills, their pickup work at the Reservoir, and their recovery work at the Tavern-on-the-Green. The challenge is to sort out who's for show and who's for place, and clothes are an easy indicator. If everything's color-coordinated—stripes on the shirt match stripes on the shoes, mascara matches sweat sox, purple punk-rock hair coincides with *le toute ensemble*, and the quads look soft—you can bet that person is into Running Fashions. The tipoff is if he or she runs the Reservoir. As recently as 1977, the Reservoir was a perfectly respectable track for serious runners. Fritz Mueller, Isabelle Carmichael, Mike Koenig, and Liz Levy trained around the Reservoir. Now, however, it has become a circular singles bar, and the main reason to jog there is to pick up or to be picked up for one-night runs. Central Park's serious runners are fairly status conscious, and the Reservoir offers no standing whatsoever. Real runners would only stop by on the occasion of a really brilliant skyline sunset, or if some injury called for a comfortable surface. (But repeated circlings of the far north loop—The Great Hill and The Mount—get approving notices.)

At the risk of overstating the obvious, the runner's Central Park is a basic 6-mile Road loop (A + B + D + F + G) with a choice of looping variations: a 1.57-mile reservoir loop; a 1.66-mile reservoir bridle-path loop; a 1.72-mile south loop (F + E); a 4-mile middle loop (A + C + D + E + G); a 1.42-mile north hill loop (B + C) and as much cross-country as free-lancers care to devise inside a 6-mile rectangle, which has a sidewalk perimeter of 6.1 miles.

FOOTING: Fairly smooth New York City asphalt on roads; potholes circled in white or yellow paint; road turtlebacked; the Reservoir track is dirt-and-cinder, and tends to unevenness, ruts, muck after a rain, frozen ridges in winter;

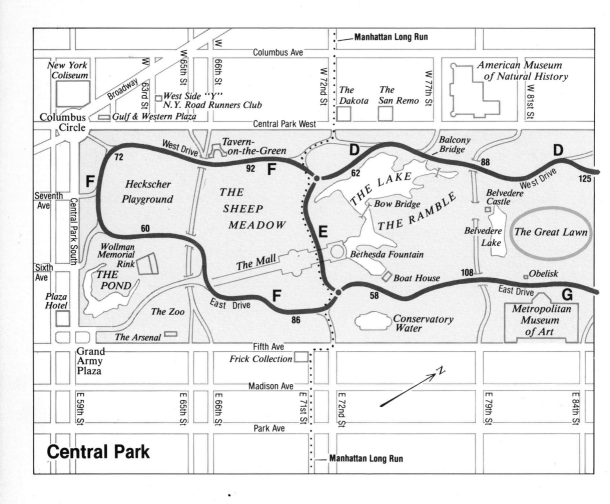

Central Park

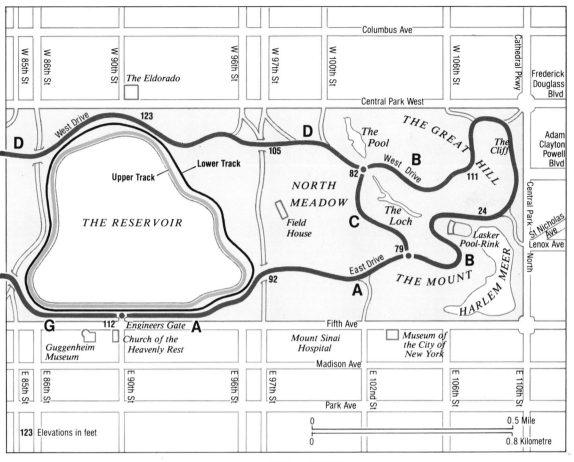

Table of Distances

A	.77				
B	1.15	**E**	.31	Reservoir Upper Track	1.57
C	.27	**F**	1.41	Reservoir Lower Track	1.66
D	1.71	**G**	1.00	Great Lawn Oval	.55

CENTRAL PARK—MEASURED COURSES

2 miles	A + B	**plus** .08 mile
3 miles	A + B + C + A	**plus** .04 mile
4 miles	A + C + D + E + G	minus .06 mile
5 miles	A + C + D + F + G	minus .16 mile
5 miles	E + G + A + B + D	**plus** .06 mile
6 miles	A + B + D + F + G	minus .04 mile
8 miles	A + B + D + F + G + A + B	**plus** .04 mile
10 miles	A + B + D + F + G + A + B + D + E	**plus** .02 mile
12 miles	(A + B + D + F + G) x 2	minus .08 mile

Bridle Path provides extremely uneven surface of dirt, with rocks, ruts, tree roots, erosion, and sloughs after a rain.

COURSE DIRECTIONS: The Park Drive can be picked up anywhere, though popular entrances are the Engineer's Gate at East Ninetieth, East Seventy-second, along Central Park South, Columbus Circle, Tavern-on-the-Green, West Seventy-second, and West Ninety-sixth. The entrance for the Reservoir on the East Side is at East Ninetieth, on the West Side at Eighty-sixth, Ninety-sixth, and 100th.

OTHER RUNS: 1) The Great Lawn measures .55 mile and is marked for speed work at 220 yards, 440 yards, 660 yards, and 880 yards. 2) The Reservoir loop measures 1.57 miles. 3) The Reservoir bridle path measures 1.66 miles.

HAZARDS: Rapists sometimes disguised as runners, especially in the wooded and less crowded north end of the park; muggers; unleashed dogs; flashers sometimes in running drag; flying wedges of bicycles; wild skateboarders; thieves who will make off with shirts, jackets, clothing shed for later pickup; horses (the bridle path is prohibited to runners, and the sign says "Bridle Path: Danger Horses Only"); also carriage horses are sometimes terrified by mobs of runners and bolt; except for the 1.72-mile south loop, it is a good idea for women runners not to work out alone in Central Park. Women should never run alone in deserted areas or at night. Much night running is done around the park, but it should be in company.

COMFORTS: Rest rooms throughout the park (Zoo, Ninety-sixth Street Field House, tennis courts, Seventy-second Street Boat House, skating rinks); fountains throughout the park (many broken); 10 A.M. Saturday N.Y.R.R.C. running clinic at Ninetieth and Fifth Avenue—group stretching, group running with knowledgeable leaders. Saturday at 10:30 A.M. and 7 P.M. Monday Race Walking clinic, Ninetieth and Fifth Avenue. The Church of the Heavenly Rest at Ninetieth and Fifth provides an earthly refuge post-race in the cold weather months. The Tavern-on-the-Green serves a "Joggers and Runners Breakfast" every morning between 7 A.M. and 9 A.M. "at minimal cost." Running clothes, post-run, are acceptable..

MASS TRANSPORT: D, A, B, C, AA, or Seventh Avenue I.R.T. local to Columbus Circle; Lexington Avenue I.R.T. to any stop between Fifty-ninth Street and 110th. Walk west.

EXTENSIONS: 1) From East Seventy-second and the Park Drive run east to the pedestrian bridge onto the East River Jogging Path for 1.14 miles. 2) From West Seventy-second and Central Park West run west to Riverside Park for .63 mile.

RIVERSIDE PARK

5.5 miles, Seventy-second Street to the George Washington Bridge

At Seventy-second Street, the beginning of the Riverside excursion, the runner is confronted with the choice of three routes: run it on the upper level, Riverside Drive; run it on the middle level, the Terrace; run it on the river level, by the Hudson. (A fourth possibility is to interlace parts of all three for hill workouts on the east-west paths.) The Riverside runs are linear, like the park, which was designed on three levels by Frederick Law Olmsted, in 1873.

Riverside Drive is the most popular of the routes, the one followed by the herd of Thursday night Bridge Runners and theoretically the safest one—though safety, particularly for women, is not one of the park's principal virtues. Here the sidewalk is wide, and the elm-shaded promenade has a gracious European look and feel to it, despite the habit of many of the bench warmers to bring along their disco tape decks. The Drive doesn't have style, it has styles; and if you run it often enough you will learn to tell from Art Deco and Beaux Arts. Handsome, overdone, underdone brownstones and limestones, as well as imposing apartment buildings, line the Drive. The key-on here, or at least the magic, is in approaching the awesome suspension of the George Washington Bridge at a run, the challenge in the undulating ridge path. Riverside Drive runners look to be a fairly sober lot—T-shirts in the Zabar's, Mostly Mozart, New York City Ballet range—intellectuals of high cardiovascular caliber.

The Riverside Park mid-level—the Terrace—takes you along an inland esplanade, through once formal, now derelict and informal, gardens and allées, where you may test yourself against a measured mile. This level ends at the 122nd Street tennis courts, after two miles, but hill work is always possible. The Terrace is more secluded than either the Drive or the river route and less windy. Some bag ladies take the sun here, but you will find few running ladies on this level, and none but the very reckless running alone. Triple buddy system recommended.

The river path is the quietest and least frequented of the three routes, especially in its northern reaches past 100th. Runners tired of circling Central Park can run straight up beside the Hudson. You approach the George Washington at the humble level of its feet, and so slowly that its growth on you seems almost natural. The ravages of Superman hit the park in 1937, when Robert Moses managed to appropriate a good part of it on behalf of the automobile, transforming it into the Henry Hudson Parkway. At certain places toward 125th on the river route, the park (not the parkway) is thin enough to be diagnosed consumptive, the automobile close enough to ruin the serenity, and the path a dangerous defile.

FOOTING: Riverside Drive sidewalk is asphalt tile, surface is quite uneven; narrow asphalt strip on western edge has a share of potholes and cracks; toward the bridge, sidewalk degenerates to dirt-pebble-glass mess, broken up by roots and erosion. The Terrace is a choice of grass, dirt, asphalt, some con-

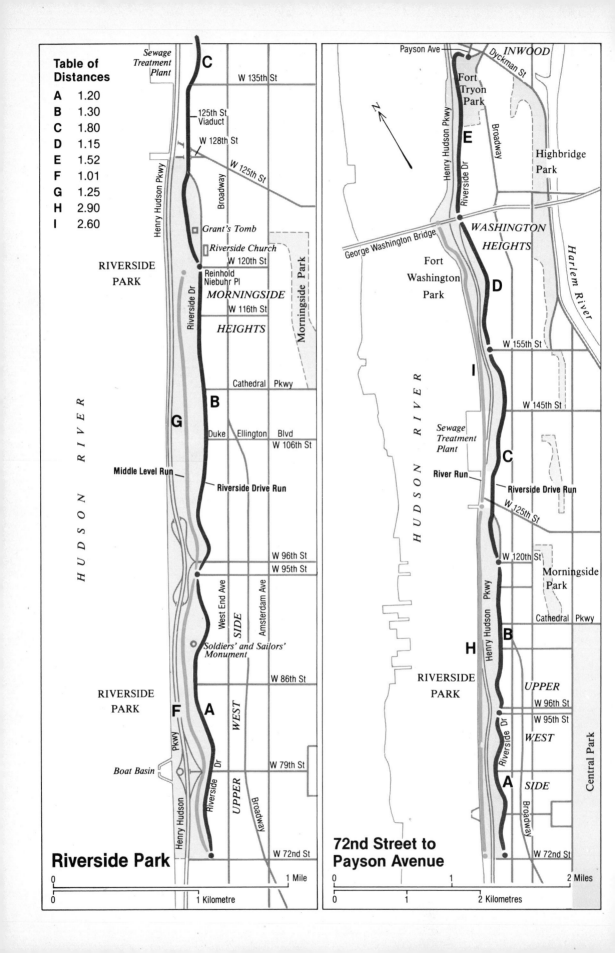

Table of Distances

A	1.20
B	1.30
C	1.80
D	1.15
E	1.52
F	1.01
G	1.25
H	2.90
I	2.60

Left map:

Sewage Treatment Plant

C

W 135th St

Henry Hudson Pkwy

125th St Viaduct

W 128th St

Broadway

W 125th St

RIVERSIDE PARK

Grant's Tomb

Riverside Church

W 120th St

Reinhold Niebuhr Pl

Riverside Dr

MORNINGSIDE

W 116th St

HEIGHTS

Morningside Park

Cathedral Pkwy

B

G

Duke Ellington Blvd

W 106th St

Middle Level Run

Riverside Drive Run

HUDSON RIVER

W 96th St

W 95th St

West End Ave

Amsterdam Ave

SIDE

Soldiers' and Sailors' Monument

W 86th St

RIVERSIDE PARK

F **A**

WEST

Pkwy

Boat Basin

Riverside Dr

UPPER

W 79th St

Henry Hudson

Broadway

W 72nd St

Riverside Park

0   1 Mile

0   1 Kilometre

Right map:

Payson Ave

INWOOD

Dyckman St

Fort Tryon Park

E

Henry Hudson Pkwy

Broadway

Riverside Dr

Highbridge Park

WASHINGTON

George Washington Bridge

HEIGHTS

Harlem River

Fort Washington Park

D

W 155th St

HUDSON RIVER

I

W 145th St

Sewage Treatment Plant

C

River Run

Riverside Drive Run

W 125th St

Morningside Park

W 120th St

Henry Hudson Pkwy

Cathedral Pkwy

H **B**

RIVERSIDE PARK

UPPER

W 96th St

W 95th St

Riverside Dr

WEST

Central Park

A *SIDE*

Broadway

W 72nd St

72nd Street to Payson Avenue

0   1   2 Miles

0   1   2 Kilometres

N

crete—fairly smooth. River path begins on asphalt, followed by segments of dirt and asphalt; below 125th, eroded dirt above seawall, some sizable holes—watch out for them.

COURSE DIRECTIONS: Pick up Riverside Drive at Seventy-second, stay on sidewalk, going north, till drive passes under the George Washington Bridge (A + B + C + D). Middle level run begins at the same place. Take the asphalt path that angles left and dips into the park. Continue north on what is obviously the middle way, crossing Seventy-ninth and Ninety-sixth en route, till stopped by tennis courts (F + G) below Riverside Church. Stairs up right lead to Riverside Drive. For the river level, take path west from 72nd and Riverside; pass through a tunnel and go right, then left to the river promenade; head north beside the river. Beyond 125th, it is sometimes possible to stay beside the river, but occasionally gates to the sewage-treatment plant at 135th are locked and you must climb the long flight of stairs at 136th to Riverside Drive. Stairs at 148th will return you to the river path (H + I).

OTHER RUNS: A 220-yard cinder track at Seventy-fourth Street, just above the start of the Riverside promenade.

HAZARDS: Unleashed muggers and rapists at all times of day and night; *always* risky for lone women runners (Riverside Drive route as well), group running recommended; some air pollution from Riverside Drive traffic and Henry Hudson Parkway; dogs off leash; harsh winter winds off the Hudson; kids on bicycles and Big Wheels; in summer, poison ivy lines narrow river path below 125th; occasional rats along river; isolated areas of woods and tall bushes along northern segment of Riverside Drive and river path.

COMFORTS: Occasional water fountains (usually nonfunctional); a few Parks Department rest rooms, generally closed.

MASS TRANSPORT: Seventh Avenue I.R.T. express to West Seventy-second Street and walk west two blocks to Riverside Park; Eighth Avenue I.N.D. A train to 175th and Fort Washington Avenue and walk west. Street parking available at both ends.

EXTENSIONS: 1) From Riverside Drive and the George Washington Bridge continue north 1.5 miles to Riverside Drive at Payson (E)—Inwood Hill Park to your left, Fort Tryon Park to your right. 2) To run the 1.27-mile George Washington Bridge, leave Riverside Drive on the 181st Street exit road, right; go behind the metal railing on right, before the bridge supports; a concrete ramp leads up from the sidewalk and zigzags the hillside to 177th Street; right onto 177th; left onto Cabrini Boulevard; left onto 178th; left onto G.W. Bridge walkway ramp, south side of bridge. 3) For the 6.25-mile run to South Ferry, go south at the Seventy-second Street river edge of the park. A dirt road leads through the railroad yards there, and leaves you under the Westside Highway at Sixtieth. From there, you can pick your way south beside West Street.

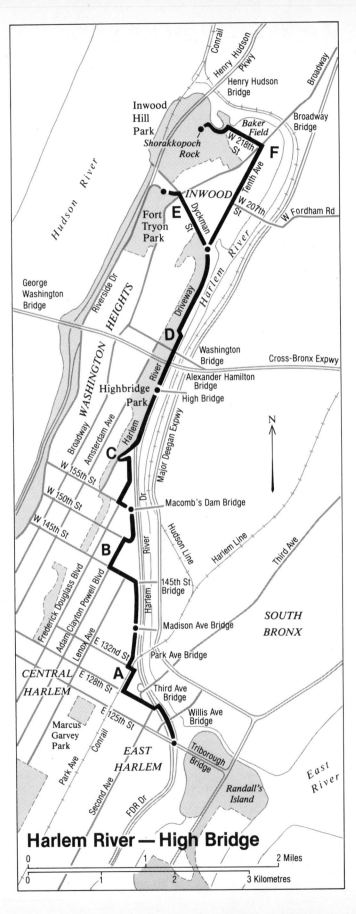

Harlem River — High Bridge

Table of Distances	
A	1.26
B	1.26
C	1.24
D	1.26
E	.67
F	1.67

HARLEM RIVER—HIGH BRIDGE

5 miles

The trickiest five miles of the 31-mile Manhattan Long Run, this stretch of upper Manhattan should be considered a running link, not a run to be done for its own sake. Navigation of this course would occur not to the average pedestrian but only to the sort of long, long distance devotee who will attempt any passage in the pursuit of distance without repetition.

South to north, the scenery includes the Park Avenue E l, acres of burned-out buildings, the long-lived Harlem River Houses (1937; N.Y.C.'s first federally built, funded, and owned project) between West 151st and 153rd, and after 2.5 miles, Highbridge Park, named for the High Bridge that carried Croton Aqueduct water across the Harlem River in the nineteenth century.

In 1888, Calvert Vaux and Samuel Parsons, Jr., designed a ridge park at the western end of the bridge. Highbridge Park is more vertical than horizontal, and the spine is so steep that it cannot be run, except by quadrupeds or snakes. The occasional Highbridge runner, therefore, treads the deep valley skirt of the park beside the Harlem River and Harlem River Driveway.

FOOTING: Flat, mostly on asphalt road or asphalt path beside river; some concrete-sidewalk stretches and curbs; a beach of broken glass.

COURSE DIRECTIONS: Begin at riverside path under the Triborough Bridge at 125th Street; go north beside the river for two and a half blocks; run left (look carefully) across the Harlem River Drive access road where a chain link fence around a children's playground has been taken down; cross the playground and head west on 128th; go right on Park Avenue; at 132nd go left across Park Avenue (A) and right immediately onto the service road beside the Harlem River Drive; continue north to 145th; at Lenox go left on 145th; right onto Adam Clayton Powell Boulevard; right at 150th and Adam Clayton Powell into the Harlem River Houses park; left before the comfort station which may still have a black astronaut painted on it, down a ramp and left into a narrow granite-cobbled pass north; left onto 155th Street (B); right onto Frederick Douglass Boulevard and pass Ralph Rangel Houses; left 200 yards uphill, then right across road and switchback onto Harlem River Driveway ramp; careful here, sidewalk narrow; right at bottom of ramp onto path north beside Harlem River; left, with care, and cross Harlem River Driveway at grade where asphalt path ends; right on path beside Highbridge Park (C + D), to its most northern point at Dyckman and Nagle Avenue.

HAZARDS: Cars on the service road between 132nd and 155th, as well as mini-motorcycles and bicycles operated by kids; speeding automobiles at those places where you must ford the road, especially at the access ramp to the Harlem River Driveway and the crossing of the Drive itself near the High Bridge; bad exhaust pollution on windless days; not safe for women running alone, and not at all safe for anyone at night.

MASS TRANSPORT: Lexington Avenue I.R.T. 4, 5, 6 to 125th and Lexington and walk east; Seventh Avenue I.R.T. 2 or 3 to 125th and Lenox and walk east; I.R.T. No. 1 to Dyckman Street; I.N.D. Eighth Avenue A train to Dyckman Street.

EXTENSION: To Shorakkopoch Rock (F), continue north on Tenth Avenue from the junction of Dyckman and the Harlem River Driveway to West 218th; left onto 218th past Baker Field and pick up the park path west to the Rock.

FORT TRYON PARK–CLOISTERS

2 miles, hill loops
1 mile, Cloisters loop (Margaret Corbin Drive)

Fort Tryon is for the strong of quad. The Fort's hills are steep, on a par with those in Inwood Hill Park, rise to 267 feet, and are impossible to avoid. The Fort retains its Tory name, donated by William Tryon, New York's British governor when the revolution broke out. Fort Tryon, a Hessian bluffhold during the revolution, is guaranteed to wear you out, break down your resistance. It's a good place to impress yourself with your cardiovascular prowess, so save it for when you're feeling strong.

Fort Tryon has far more serious walkers than runners. On weekends, the semiformal gardens along the entry ridge, landscaped by Frederick Law Olmsted, Jr., are crowded with elderly Europeans strolling in sturdy walking shoes, and English is rarely heard. You might make the Cloisters the goal of your run, looping the heights and hillsides for several miles before cooling off in their stone corridors, say in the twelfth-century cloister of St. Michel de Cuxa or in the slightly older cloister of St. Guilhem-le-Désert. In circling the Cloisters, you are running around the Metropolitan Museum's medieval collection, including the six Unicorn Tapestries, into which a good deal of fifteenth-century running was loomed.

For novices who want the atmosphere without the strain, there is the fairly gentle 1-mile Margaret Corbin Drive, the auto loop of the Cloisters.

FOOTING: Most paths are of old, soft asphalt, somewhat chewed away at the edges; some flights of stairs; extremely steep hills.

COURSE DIRECTIONS: Begin at Payson Avenue–Riverside Drive entrance; take first right up long, steep, switchback hill (A); turn right onto first path at top which runs south below the Cloisters roadway; cross bridge over rock cut (B); turn right onto first path after bridge and keep to river side of the hill; at next path dip right and down, circle a lawn, then run up and left; where path crosses another take a right; at the 190th Street–Washington Avenue entrance (C) turn left and run the straight garden path to Overlook Terrace; promenade curves right; take the stairs down at north end; go left for a short distance (D), then right through a small tunnel and straight on a wooded path; go left at first intersection and head downhill; near bottom of hill take the path to right that winds up the back side of the Cloisters hill, ending near the Cloisters front entrance (E). Or return to Payson Avenue (A) for the full 2 miles.

HAZARDS: Generally safe for women running alone, though paths on the back side of the hills, facing inland, are quite deserted and wooded, and lone running there is not recommended; perilous night running.

COMFORTS: Fountains throughout park, on Overlook Terrace, near rock-cut bridge and children's playground at Broadway and Riverside Drive, where there are rest rooms; fountains and rest rooms in the Cloisters.

MASS TRANSPORT: Take the I.N.D. Eighth Avenue A train to Overlook Terrace–190th Street or to 200th Street–Dyckman Street; M4 or M100 bus; some parking available at Cloisters.

INWOOD HILL PARK

2.62 miles, Shorakkopoch Trail
1.67 miles, Bengtson's Hill
1.6 miles, River Run

Inwood Hill Park is so far north in Manhattan you think it must be the Bronx. All that remains of Manhattan's primeval forest and almost all of Manhattan's hills are here. The corkscrew-shaped course poses a strenuous variety of hill challenges, gradients gradual and steep, short, long, and switchbacked. For serious hill workouts, when your resistance is high, Inwood Hill is the place.

It isn't often in the city that you have the chance to run on Indian paths. Though the ones in Inwood Hill are asphalt-paved, the trees carry signs warning "Natural Trail, Caution." The keystone of the Inwood Hill run, and a ritual starting place for many, is the Shorakkopoch Rock, once part of an Algonquin village, and the place where, in 1626, Peter Minuit bought Manhattan Island for trinkets and beads. The park's highest point, the 232.75-foot Overlook, commands the Palisades and the Hudson upriver beyond the Tappan Zee Bridge and downriver far beyond the George Washington.

Trails through Inwood Hill's grandly forested interior, as well as Fort Tryon's back side, present hackberries, mulberries, blueberries, grapes, and wild cherries, in season, to those prone to snacking on the run. For those whose running has caused them to bird, the birding includes pheasants, indigo buntings, scarlet tanagers, flickers, and a red-tailed hawk. The wildness of the wildflowers goes to Dutchman's breeches, the towering trees to ancient oaks and beeches.

Inwood Hill still qualifies for the 1939 W.P.A. designation "wildest 167 acres in Manhattan," and people have been reported to be living year round in the Indian Caves there. Inwood Hill remains Manhattan's last wilderness (despite Robert Moses' partial desecration in 1936, when he found it cheaper to cut the Henry Hudson Parkway through it), relatively unfrequented and run mostly by a small crew of neighborhood runners. The Thoreauvian runner who lacks the gas to drive to the country might happily subway to Inwood Hill for the preservation of a small part of the world and the sake of both quads.

FOOTING: Mostly old asphalt trail, rather soft, decaying and ragged at the edges; a few stretches of new asphalt; some small gullies, steep grades, and unforgiving climbs to the Overlook; in winter, extremely dangerous iced patches near the Henry Hudson Bridge and on the cliffside trail between Shorakkopoch Rock and the bridge; serious erosion on downhill side of path between Payson Avenue and the Rock, where the asphalt has decayed and the dirt beneath it washed out, such that a leg through one of these holes could break; stairs over railroad tracks and at several places in the wood.

COURSE DIRECTIONS: Shorakkopoch Trail—Begin on the path northeast of the Payson Avenue playground (F); climb a flight of stairs; turn right at small circle at top of stairs; turn right onto path that leaves an immense cracked rock to left; continue straight along the Clove, past three paths, to the Shorakkopoch Rock (G). From the Rock head west; take the first path right up

Fort Tryon Park — Inwood Hill Park

Table of Distances

A	.30
B	.25
C	.35
D	.35
E	.45
F	.25
G	.57
H	.30
I	.40
J	.79
K	.56
L	.24
M	.23
N	.20
O	.37
P	.20

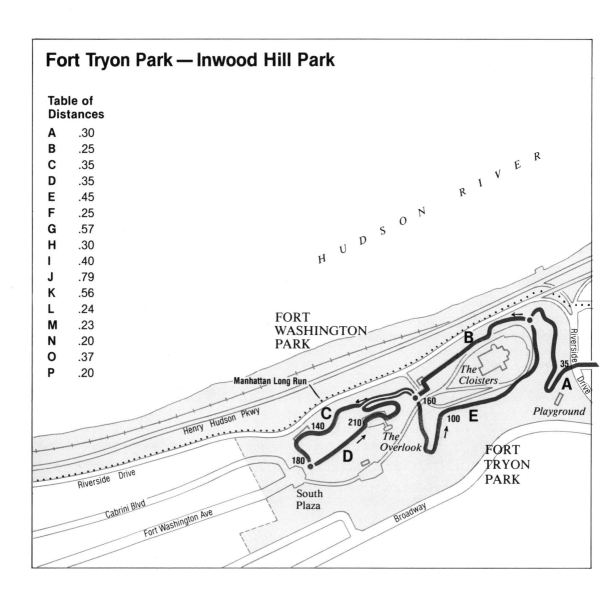

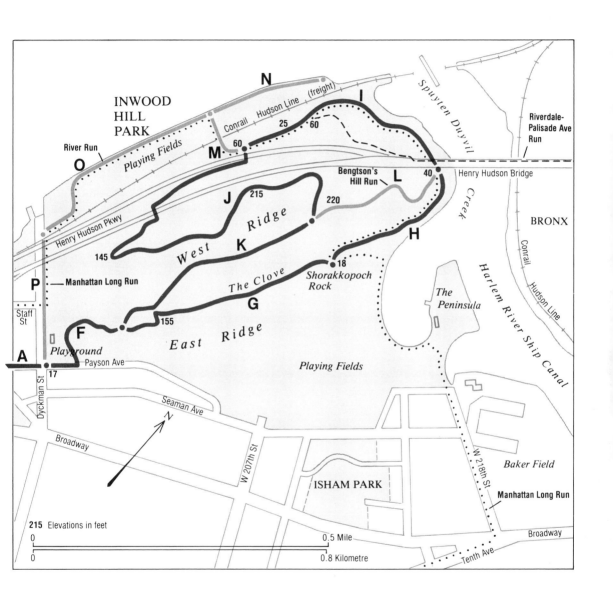

INWOOD
HILL
PARK

N

Conrail Hudson Line (freight)

I

Spuyten Duyvil

Riverdale-
Palisade Ave
Run

River Run

O

Playing Fields

25   60

M   60

Bengtson's
Hill Run

L

40   Henry Hudson Bridge

Creek

BRONX

J   215

West   Ridge

K

220

Bengtson's

H

Conrail

Hudson Line

145

P   — Manhattan Long Run

The Clove

Shorakkopoch
Rock

18

The
Peninsula

Harlem River Ship Canal

Staff
St

F

155

G

East   Ridge

Playground

A   17

Payson Ave

Dyckman St

Seaman Ave

N

Playing Fields

Broadway

W 207th St

ISHAM PARK

W 218th St

Baker Field

Manhattan Long Run

215 Elevations in feet

Broadway

0

0.5 Mile

0

0.8 Kilometre

Tenth Ave

a steep hill that overlooks the Spuyten Duyvil Creek to a fork beneath the Henry Hudson Bridge (H); follow path to the right under bridge and around the hillside to a trail branching left leading to a set of steps (I); pass through a brick tunnel under the lower level of the Henry Hudson Parkway; after the tunnel, take the slate steps to the right; follow path through a second brick tunnel; pick up the asphalt path on the far side and continue to the second asphalt path turnoff; turn left at junction where path is defined by granite cobblestones; continue uphill; turn left onto the second path and climb at a steeper grade to the Overlook; after looking, stay on asphalt path to left, which will curve right after cresting the ridge and cross another path, dead ending shortly thereafter (J); take a sharp right; run down a gentle hill; ignore seven small paths (chances to turn right); go right on the eighth path, at a triangle of greenery; path curves right and then left; run down a flight of broad cement stairs; continue straight, cross path at bottom of stairs; bear left and return to Payson Avenue playground (K).

Bengtson's Hill—(Named for the Reverend William Bengtson, who once devoted an article in *The New York Times* to a description of his daily battle with this monster.) Begin at the Shorakkopoch Rock; at the fork at the top of the first hill under the Henry Hudson Bridge (H) turn left; ignore three paths to the left and one to the right as you struggle up the sternest hill in Manhattan; you will be deceived by switchbacks into thinking the climb is over; after .53 mile and many optical end-deceptions, the path intersects with the Shorakkopoch Trail (L); proceed as already directed.

The River Run: Begin at the pedestrian footpath on the west side, lower level, of the Henry Hudson Bridge; path drops down southwest through the woods (I) turn right and climb stairs to cross a railroad trestle; descend stairs to the riverine flats of Inwood Hill Park (M). You can run beside the Hudson to the north end of the park (N), turn back south to Dyckman Street and Riverside Drive (N + O + P) for 1.6 miles.

HAZARDS: Summer problems include poison ivy reaching out from trailside, bee stings, mosquitoes, and brush fires in the very dry weather; wild dogs in a pack; the occasional rat; regarded as one of New York's safest parks, in which lone women runners, elderly strollers, and women pushing prams have been observed; some broken glass; no night running.

COMFORTS: Water fountains by Columbia University's Baker Field and at park buildings in playground at Payson Avenue and Dyckman Street, near the roller rink on the river run and at ball fields; rest rooms at Payson Avenue playground.

MASS TRANSPORT: I.N.D. Eighth Avenue A train to Dyckman Street or 207th or 200th; I.R.T. No. 1 to 242nd Street–Broadway, to Dyckman Street or to 207th; M100 or Bx10 bus; street parking available.

EXTENSION: From the west side, lower level of the Henry Hudson Bridge, head north across the bridge into the Bronx for the .7-mile connecting run that joins the 2.63-mile Riverdale Run at Independence and Palisade Avenue.

EAST RIVER—
WARD'S & RANDALL'S ISLANDS

9.6 miles, South Ferry to 125th Street
13.46 miles, South Ferry–103rd—Ward's and Randall's Islands—Triborough Bridge—124th at Second Avenue

This is *the* run for the Long Polluted Distance aficionado. For a good part of the way, you're hyperventilating just inches from six lanes of internally combusting engines. The only thing less appealing than running beside the East River (and its Drive) would be swimming in it. The East River Run begins promisingly enough at South Ferry. You rendezvous head-on with Manhattan, then sneak up on and go under the great harp wires of the Brooklyn Bridge, passing the small nineteenth-century enclave of the South Street Seaport, the Wall Street profile, and the naturally-smelly Fulton Fish Market.

The East River is for the most part a rundown run with about as much visual charm as the Industrial Revolution, but it does attain a certain cruising chic along the Upper East River Drive. At Sixty-third the handwriting on the asphalt announces the 3.25-mile East River Jogging Path, which is heavily used at all hours. The promenade portion of this run, around Carl Schurz Park, is formally called the John Finley Walk after a past editor-in-chief of the *Times* who was one of the city's most notable and most enthusiastic pedestrians. (Informally, it's also called the Jill Clayburgh *An Unmarried Woman* Jog, for the film that shot its runs here.) After the Reservoir, this is the place to be seen among a certain soft core segment of New York's running population. The ambiance is that of an Upper East Side singles bar, where the togged joggers—color-coordinated couples, satin running outfits, running pickups, even running mascara—are on parade and do the disco distance.

Running upstream to 103rd you can fix on the orange, pink, and purple modestly psychedelic Ward's Island Pedestrian Bridge—your chance to run a rainbow with an island at its end. A loop through the tall grass and unkempt meadows of Ward's—not named for foundlings, but for the brothers Ward who farmed the acerage in the 1790's—is 1.75 miles long and remarkably rustic. (Big-city campers pitch their tents here overnight.)

Randall's Island, now the Siamese twin of Ward's due to the landfill that has eliminated the channel between them, lacks the bucolic charm of Ward's. It is a drab, depressing landscape of vandalized park and greensward. Still, Randall's offers a 2.5-mile loop and bankside views of the Hell Gate collision of the East and Harlem Rivers.

FOOTING: Variations on the themes of asphalt (mostly with potholes), concrete, dirt, pebbled dirt, asphalt tile; a few ramps and staircases. Flat.

COURSE DIRECTIONS: Pick up South Street at South Ferry, head north beside East River on the side of the road; gladly hop onto sidewalk where it finally begins at Montgomery Street (Pier 36) (A + B); continue north on promenade beside river in East River Park (C); at East Thirteenth (perilously narrow path) continue north beside the East River Drive; at East Twenty-third

(D) go left one block; right onto Asser Levy Place (pass old public baths); left on-to East Twenty-fifth; right onto First Avenue; north on First Avenue and under Queensboro Bridge; right on Sixtieth; cross York Avenue, go up heliport drive and left down to marked beginning of East River Jogging Path (E + F); continue north beside river (the New York City Marathon passed this way in 1976, and remnants of the blue line remain). You can continue north beside the river to stairs at Eighty-first (G), or at East Seventy-eighth follow the blue line up a pedestrian ramp and over the Drive, passing Cherokee Place; right onto York, right onto Eighty-first, cross East End Avenue, climb a flight of stairs, and left for the singles half mile on the Finley–Schurz–Clayburgh promenade (H). Continue north beside the river to 125th beneath the Triborough (J), or, at 103rd (I), cross over to Ward's Island on the pedestrian bridge; leaving the footbridge, go right and follow path that more or less parallels the shore; keep right, cross under the Triborough, and continue up a hill; on hilltop, asphalt dead ends before a chain link fence of the Manhattan Psychiatric Center; tending right is a path through the grass leading to a big hole in the fence about a hundred yards before the Hell Gate railroad bridge (K); run left under the bridge supports past illegal garbage dumps and pick up rutted dirt road that soon turns right and fuses with an asphalt road. Continue on asphalt road to gatehouse for the bridge to Randall's Island; on Randall's (L), go right on road and, two street lamps after the Fire Academy, go right on an asphalt path; go left at lamp post RIX 4-3 (the number appears at the base of the post), then right on the asphalt path that parallels the shore—all the while passing under bridges—until the path returns you to the bridge to Ward's Island (M); the pedestrian walkway to Manhattan on the Triborough can be found on the west-central part of the island, north of Downing Stadium; exit is at 124th and Second Avenue (N).

OTHER RUNS: All-weather 440-yard track in Downing Stadium on Randall's Island offers the best running surface in New York City; permit required.

HAZARDS: The automobile: lead and carbon-monoxide inhalation from too-close proximity, the need to cross streets and run in streets in many places, the narrow defiles between cars and the turbulent East River; sections of glassy pavement; night running O.K. along 3.25-mile East River Jogging Path with caution, but not on rest of route; women runners are advised not to run Ward's and Randall's alone.

COMFORTS: Occasional water fountains at Battery Park, East River Park, Carl Schurz Park; rest rooms at South Ferry.

MASS TRANSPORT: Seventh Avenue I.R.T. local to South Ferry; Seventh Avenue I.R.T. express to 125th and Lenox and walk east; Lexington Avenue I.R.T. No. 4 or 5 to Bowling Green and walk south; Lexington Avenue I.R.T. No. 4, 5, or 6 to 125th and walk east. Street parking at both ends of run and on Randall's Island.

EXTENSIONS: 1) At 125th and Harlem River begin the 5-mile Harlem River Run north to Fort Tryon and Inwood Hill Parks and Runs. 2) At South Ferry you can break into the 9.1-mile Battery to Brooklyn Bridge Run.

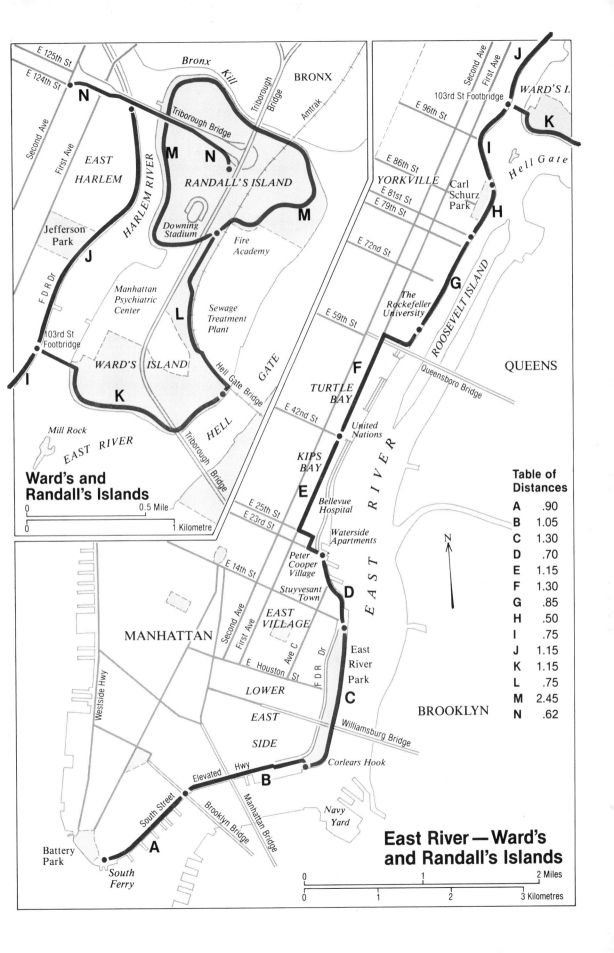

Ward's and Randall's Islands

0   0.5 Mile

0   1 Kilometre

E 125th St
E 124th St
Bronx Kill
BRONX
N
Triborough Bridge
Second Ave
First Ave
Triborough Bridge
Amtrak
M
N
EAST HARLEM
RANDALL'S ISLAND
HARLEM RIVER
M
Jefferson Park
Downing Stadium
Fire Academy
J
FDR Dr
Manhattan Psychiatric Center
Sewage Treatment Plant
L
103rd St Footbridge
WARD'S ISLAND
Hell Gate Bridge
HELL GATE
I
K
Mill Rock
EAST RIVER
Triborough Bridge

J
Second Ave
First Ave
103rd St Footbridge
WARD'S I.
E 96th St
K
YORKVILLE
Hell Gate
E 86th St
Carl Schurz Park
E 81st St
I
E 79th St
H
E 72nd St
ROOSEVELT ISLAND
G
The Rockefeller University
E 59th St
QUEENS
Queensboro Bridge
F
TURTLE BAY
E 42nd St
United Nations
EAST RIVER
KIPS BAY
Bellevue Hospital
E 25th St
E 23rd St
Waterside Apartments
E
Peter Cooper Village
MANHATTAN
E 14th St
Stuyvesant Town
D
EAST VILLAGE
East River Park
Second Ave
First Ave
Ave C
E Houston St
FDR Dr
C
LOWER
Westside Hwy
EAST
Williamsburg Bridge
BROOKLYN
SIDE
Corlears Hook
Elevated Hwy
B
South Street
Navy Yard
Brooklyn Bridge
Manhattan Bridge
Battery Park
A
South Ferry

N

Table of Distances

A	.90
B	1.05
C	1.30
D	.70
E	1.15
F	1.30
G	.85
H	.50
I	.75
J	1.15
K	1.15
L	.75
M	2.45
N	.62

East River — Ward's and Randall's Islands

0   1   2 Miles

0   1   2   3 Kilometres

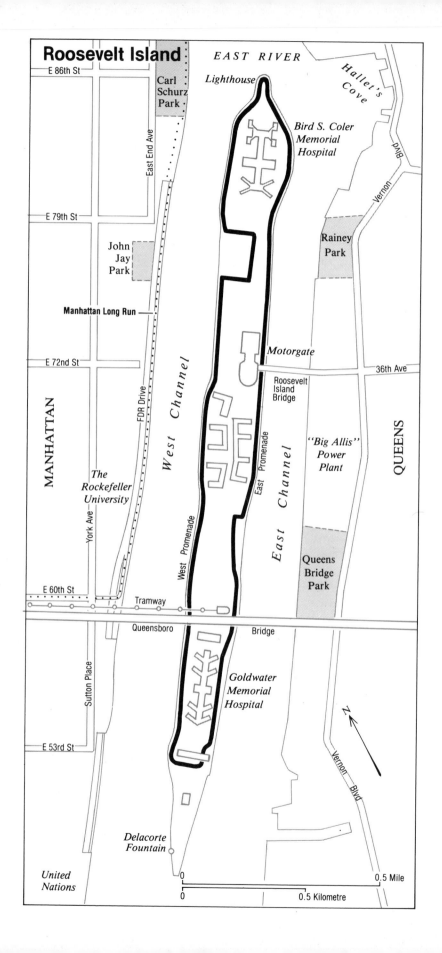

Roosevelt Island

EAST RIVER

E 86th St

Carl
Schurz
Park

Lighthouse

Hallet's
Cove

Bird S. Coler
Memorial
Hospital

East End Ave

E 79th St

Vernon Blvd

John
Jay
Park

Rainey
Park

Manhattan Long Run

Motorgate

E 72nd St

36th Ave

West Channel

Roosevelt
Island
Bridge

MANHATTAN

FDR Drive

"Big Allis"
Power
Plant

QUEENS

The
Rockefeller
University

East Promenade

East Channel

York Ave

West Promenade

Queens
Bridge
Park

E 60th St

Tramway

Queensboro   Bridge

Goldwater
Memorial
Hospital

Sutton Place

N

E 53rd St

Vernon Blvd

Delacorte
Fountain

United
Nations

0   0.5 Mile

0   0.5 Kilometre

ROOSEVELT ISLAND

3.6 miles

Other-island Manhattan: just a jog and a tram-hop from Bloomie's. Native runners wear T-shirts proclaiming "Roosevelt Island, The Little Apple." If the Urban Development Corporation had done nothing else but give New York a reason to build the aerial tram in 1976, thus making accessible this flat mid-river run, that would have been enough. The U.D.C. put up a high rise new town at the island's center, offering a democratic mix of housing for wealthy, middle-, and lower-income folks and the handicapped; planned parks for the north and south ends; and landscaped promenades on the east and west sides.

Roosevelt Island is the 1973 recycling of Welfare Island, which for nearly a century and a half held the city's penitentiary (Boss Tweed was incarcerated here), workhouse, hostels for the indigent, and hospitals for the chronically ill. From the 1630's until 1828, the island had been farmed. Two hospitals, Goldwater Memorial and Bird S. Coler, continue to treat the chronically ill here. Many patients move about the island in wheelchairs, and with them in mind the island's sidewalks were designed with ramps, instead of steps. Over the course of the last forty years the island has gained three-quarters of a mile in length and fifty feet in width, so that it is now two and a half miles by eight hundred feet.

Running Roosevelt Island is about as close as you can come to running *on* the water. It might be likened to running the deck of the world's largest super-tanker, joining the river traffic that seems to include tugs, barges, sails, and freighters at all hours.

Runners, like computers, are forever keying on things. Running north on Roosevelt Island they can key on some of the eighteenth- and nineteenth-century remains of Old New York—an almost two-hundred-year-old farmhouse, the 1839 Octagon Tower (formerly the New York City Lunatic Asylum), and a century-old stone lighthouse (said to have been built by one of the island's resident lunatics). Running south they can key on the Queensboro Bridge and pass directly *under* Mile 16 of the New York City Marathon and the stacks of Big Allis, Con Ed's temperamental turbine generator.

FOOTING: Smooth asphalt road much of the way; choice of dirt and tufted grass in places; a spiral sculpture to hop through; a few brick walkways, some concrete; very flat.

COURSE DIRECTIONS: Self-evident. Upon leaving the aerial tram, pick up the circular island road that runs next to the breakwater most of the way.

HAZARDS: Few. Private guards and good night lighting make the island safe day and night; some rats near the breakwater; a few slow-moving vehicles on the roadways; be respectful of the wheelchair trekkers on the roads and sidewalks.

MASS TRANSPORT: Aerial tram from Sixtieth and Second Avenue, which costs 50 cents and runs every 15 minutes; E, F, GG, or EE subway to Queens Plaza, and Q102 bus onto the island; or run from Queens Plaza; parking available on the island, or park in Queens.

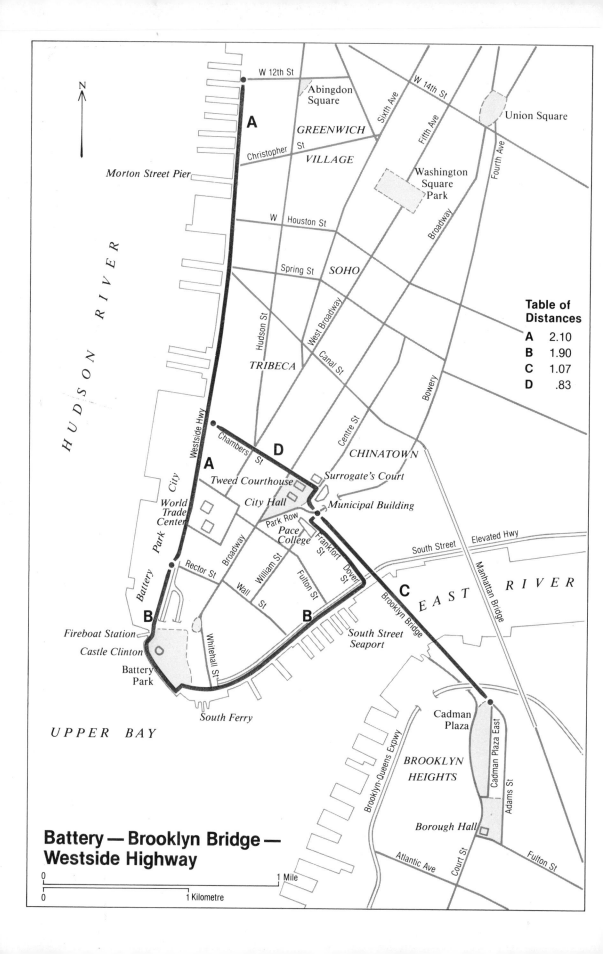

N

W 12th St

Abingdon
Square

W 14th St

Union Square

A

GREENWICH

Sixth Ave

Fifth Ave

Fourth Ave

Christopher
St

VILLAGE

Morton Street Pier

Washington
Square
Park

Broadway

W   Houston St

Spring St

SOHO

Hudson St

West Broadway

Canal St

TRIBECA

Centre St

Bowery

**Table of
Distances**

A   2.10
B   1.90
C   1.07
D   .83

Westside Hwy

Chambers
St

D

CHINATOWN

A

Tweed Courthouse

Surrogate's Court

City

City Hall

Park Row

Municipal Building

*World
Trade
Center*

Battery Park

*Pace
College*

Frankfort St

Dover St

South Street

Elevated Hwy

E A S T   *R I V E R*

Broadway

Rector St

William St

Fulton St

Brooklyn Bridge

C

Manhattan Bridge

B

Wall

St

B

*South Street
Seaport*

Fireboat Station

Castle Clinton

Whitehall St

*Battery
Park*

*Cadman
Plaza*

Cadman Plaza East

South Ferry

Brooklyn-Queens Expwy

*BROOKLYN
HEIGHTS*

Adams St

U P P E R   B A Y

H U D S O N   R I V E R

Borough Hall

**Battery — Brooklyn Bridge —
Westside Highway**

Atlantic Ave

Court St

Fulton St

0 |_____| 1 Mile

0 |_____| 1 Kilometre

BATTERY—BROOKLYN BRIDGE—WESTSIDE HIGHWAY

9.1-mile loop

The Battery to Brooklyn Bridge loop dates from the mid-seventies when the deteriorating Westside Highway was declared unsafe for the weight and speed of cars. With the mass movement to running, the route has taken on the look of a financial classic for Wall Streeters and a weekend classic for Brooklynites. This is Manhattan's harbor run and includes the two remaining downtown miles of the Westside Highway. It gives you the chance to run knee-high to some of New York's earliest skyscrapers (their tops more fanciful than financial, often garlanded with flowers), only recently dwarfed, twice, by the over-boring hundred and ten stories of the World Trade Center, which box-tops the Lower Manhattan skyline. Pointed south into a salty breeze you can try to keep pace with a liner moving down the Hudson to sea.

From Battery Park it is impossible to avoid a runner fixation on the Gothic towers and graceful catenary curves of the Brooklyn Bridge. The only expletive for the Brooklyn Bridge run is thrilling. The bridge path is like a clerestory above the city, and the view is a celebration, which probably accounts for the popularity of the run. (Also, you earn the right to drop, casually, "The other day, when I ran over the Brooklyn Bridge. . . .") Running the Brooklyn Bridge is a peak experience, on the boards, like running the vaults of a Gothic cathedral, or between the strings of a giant's harp. The Great Bridge arcs gradually, slopes gently, and drops you off in Brooklyn Heights.

FOOTING: A potpourri—concrete, asphalt, asphalt tile, stairs on the bridge, sloping boardwalk over the bridge, ramps onto the Westside Highway.

COURSE DIRECTIONS: Run can be joined anywhere, but a common starting point is the Rector Street ramp onto the Westside Highway; head north for 2.1 miles to the stop sign around Twelfth Street (A); turn back and exit where you entered (A); continue south on West Street; keep to the shoreline as you pass through Battery Park and South Ferry; head north on South Street to Dover; left on Dover (which becomes Frankfort Street); right onto William Street; after half a block right up William Street stairs (B) onto Brooklyn Bridge; continue southeast across the bridge to Brooklyn; at the bottom of the bridge stairs at Cadman Plaza East (C), turn around and cross back to Manhattan (C); leave City Hall to your left as you cut behind it and continue west across the island on Chambers Street (D); at Chambers and West—the Westside Highway.

HAZARDS: Strong winter winds make for a noticeable chill factor on the bridge and Westside Highway; exhilarating night running (all the East River bridges wear necklaces), though women should not run it alone at night.

COMFORTS: Fountains at Battery Park, South Ferry, and City Hall Park.

MASS TRANSPORT: Seventh Avenue I.R.T. local to South Ferry or Canal Street and head west; Seventh Avenue I.R.T. express to Chambers Street and walk west; Lexington Avenue No. 4 or 5 to Bowling Green and walk west.

MANHATTAN MINI-RUNS

CITY HALL PARK: Apolitical running for non candidates. You may take a .5-mile run around the city's seat of power, but best not try it on a weekday when the park's walks are crowded with civil servants and the lawns with drug dealers, winos, and derelicts. The jaunt is on the outer sidewalk which is cracked, potted, and pocked, but the water fountains *work*! There are large trees for shade; the confectionary Woolworth Building; City Hall, the Municipal Building, and the courts for formal European seriousness; and the lyrical approach to the Brooklyn Bridge. You are also running around a historical plot—the old City Common—whereon General George Washington, in July 1776, read the Declaration of Independence to his assembled troops.

WASHINGTON SQUARE PARK: Washington Square Park is the flat and intellectual four-sided .5-mile run in the Village—the N.Y.U. track as it were. Professors (as well as the university's president), students, actors, writers, et cetera run its crowded sidewalk perimeter, cheerfully dodging strollers and leashed-dog walkers, while inhaling fumes from passing heavy traffic. Frequented by running addicts at all hours, all year, it has plenty of interest for the historical running mind. Washington Square is a handy run around an old potters field (1789 to 1823), which was also a public gallows, hanging being done from the trees in a holiday atmosphere. The park dates from 1827, the Fashionable Greek Revival Old Row town houses on the north date from the 1830's, and Stanford White's Washington Square Arch, the endpiece of Fifth Avenue, dates from 1895. The buildings to the south and east house New York University, which began building, and then immediately rebuilding, itself in 1830. (N.Y.U.'s newest edifice, the red sandstone Bobst Library, by Philip Johnson, dominates the southeast corner, across from the park.)

Washington Square is perhaps New York's most literary run—passing the spot where Henry James was born and other spots where James, Edith Wharton, John Dos Passos, William Dean Howells, among others, lived and worked. If you enjoy running squares and taking your chances on the irregularities of New York sidewalks, you will like lapping Washington Square. There are several water fountains, a public lavatory, frequent impromptu concerts and sermons, and infrequent ethnic clashes in the comfortably scruffy hang-loose, run-loose Village atmosphere.

TOMPKINS SQUARE PARK: Tompkins Square Park, sixteen acres between Avenues A and B, East Seventh and Tenth, provides a .5-mile outer-sidewalk run that is mostly on uneven asphalt tile with glass. The neighborhood is as rough as the sidewalk, and not recommended for night runners or lone women runners. The north side of Tenth Street across from the park is experiencing a guarded renaissance, and the west side is holding its own, but the other sides are in full dereliction. The park is a hangout for tough-looking teen-agers, though most of the benches belong to elderly park habitués. The park is there, it can be run; the risk is yours.

GRAMERCY PARK: Gramercy Park, where the sidewalks are narrow and the pedigrees long, is not much of a run—more like a hop or a skip outside the serene grass and the dowager trees of this cast-iron fenced, private key-club park. The distance, a small and elegant .2 mile, is through an architecturally intact bit of nineteenth-century New York modeled on an English square and retaining an aristocratic reserve. The sidewalk, canted and pocked, with tight corners that are tough on the knees, appears to be a nineteenth-century work as well. Still, four-and-one-third laps make a mile, and certainly that many repetitions will mark the architecture of the 1830's indelibly on the runner's mind. Running is nothing if not repetitious. And so to be seen, four times to the Gramercy Mile: The Players, a club for actors and friends, founded by Edwin Booth in 1888 (himself still standing in bronze as Hamlet inside the park), whose building was remodeled by Stanford White, who also lived on the park between 1901 and 1906; No. 19 Gramercy Park South, former mansion of Mrs. Stuyvesant Fish, more recently the home of the late Benjamin Sonnenberg. To the west, note the carefully wrought iron balconies and porches. Frequented by neighborhood runners.

MARCUS GARVEY MEMORIAL PARK (MOUNT MORRIS PARK): Marcus Garvey offers a .8-mile run around the base of Harlem's only mountain, Mount Morris, between 120th and 124th Streets. The north, west, and south sides are part of the New York City Marathon route and take you past high Victorian brownstones of late nineteenth-century Harlem, as well as past some edificially excellent church works—one gospel church and the city's only Ethiopian Hebrew Congregation, for black Jews. There are water fountains and rest rooms in the park. In 1973, the park was renamed for Marcus Garvey, the popular black leader of the Back-to-Africa movement in the early twentieth century. The sidewalk is, as are the other sidewalks of New York City, hard.

MORNINGSIDE PARK: The best way to run Morningside Park is not to run it at all. Between Cathedral Parkway and West 123rd Street, and Manhattan and Morningside Avenues, the park has the reputation of being a war zone, where the truces are frequently violated. (Not every green square on the map is safe for running.) Designed in the 1880's by Frederick Law Olmsted and Calvert Vaux, the park is a distorted rectangle whose perimeter comes to 1.5 miles. Morningside is a rugged, even hostile area, where a ghetto-and-gown struggle has raged for years between Columbia University and the local residents. (In 1968, Columbia attempted to eat up two acres of the park with a gymnasium.) Ill will persists. Not recommended. Run here at your own high risk—few others will. I.R.T. Broadway local to 110th Street and walk east.

HUDSON RIVER MEADOW RUN: There are reports of Elysian Fields on a dirt road through the narrow strip of green between the Henry Hudson Parkway and the river, west of the railroad tracks for the mile and a half between Dyckman Street and the George Washington Bridge. Those who have been there tell of shoulder high rushes, dependable river breezes, and pheasants flushed. Access is alleged to be near the river at Dyckman Street, with egress before a cliff near the George Washington Bridge, where the 5.5-mile river run south to Seventy-second Street can be joined.

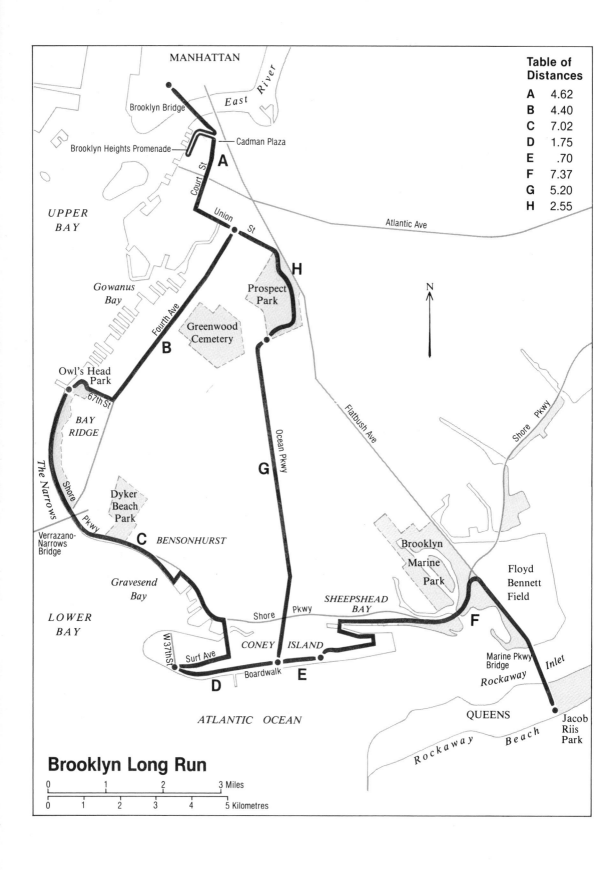

MANHATTAN

East *River*

Brooklyn Bridge

Cadman Plaza

Brooklyn Heights Promenade

A

Court St

Union St

Atlantic Ave

UPPER
BAY

**Table of
Distances**

A	4.62
B	4.40
C	7.02
D	1.75
E	.70
F	7.37
G	5.20
H	2.55

Gowanus
Bay

H

Prospect
Park

Fourth Ave

Greenwood
Cemetery

B

N

Owl's Head
Park

67th St

BAY
RIDGE

Flatbush Ave

Shore Pkwy

The Narrows

Shore

Pkwy

G

Ocean Pkwy

Dyker
Beach
Park

Verrazano-
Narrows
Bridge

C

BENSONHURST

Brooklyn
Marine
Park

Floyd
Bennett
Field

Gravesend
Bay

LOWER
BAY

Shore Pkwy

SHEEPSHEAD
BAY

F

W 37th St

Surf Ave

CONEY ISLAND

E

Marine Pkwy
Bridge

Rockaway *Inlet*

Boardwalk

D

ATLANTIC OCEAN

QUEENS

Jacob
Riis
Park

Rockaway *Beach*

Brooklyn Long Run

| 0 | 1 | 2 | 3 Miles |

| 0 | 1 | 2 | 3 | 4 | 5 Kilometres |

BROOKLYN

Brooklyn running tends to be flat, like Flatbush, and fun, like Coney Island. If Manhattan running has the reputation, as do its runners, of being intense, then Brooklyn running is laid back. While some say that Brooklyn running is merely a species of Long Island running, it is done amid the Brooklynese. Some kid on the street is bound to ask the obvious "Youse runnin'?" and then "Can I run witch youse?" In the Orthodox Jewish areas, particularly Williamsburg, the bare legs of female runners cause heads to turn—away.

The tempo of life, including running life, changes halfway across the Brooklyn Bridge. Brooklyn's streets don't run straight the way streets do in Manhattan, and Brooklyn's nineteenth-century character in architecture has survived the twentieth far more intact than Manhattan's, perhaps because it has always been primarily a residential borough. Nineteenth-century-style street-runs on the one-way lanes of neighborhoods such as Brooklyn Heights, Fort Greene, and Park Slope are fairly safe for the foot explorer, and the architecture is a silent running commentary on the look and atmosphere of old New York. Brooklyn has only one skyscraper, the Williamsburgh Savings Bank clock tower. It would not scrape anything in Manhattan, but stands twenty shoulders above the rest of Brownstone Brooklyn. Because of this there are no sky cutoffs here, and no canyons. The Brooklyn runner is *intime* with New York City's famous Big Sky and can enjoy some of the city's most brilliant pollution sunsets from the paths along its shores, its bridges, and its parks.

Twelve of the first thirteen miles of the New York City Marathon belong to the ethnic villages of Brooklyn. Brooklyn being the Borough of Churches —and therefore of steeples, many faced with clocks—marathoners and Brooklyn regulars have discovered that there is no reason to run with a watch here. Indeed, you can tell the time for miles around by the Williamsburgh Bank's four-faced clock tower. Also in Brooklyn the runner can almost always find a steeple for orientation, but, lacking that, he or she can always search the backup skyline across the river and pick up one of Manhattan's skyscrapers—the World Trade Twins, say, or the Chrysler Building—for guidance.

Brooklyn is also a borough of great bridges, the Brooklyn, with its bridge-walk boardwalk; the Manhattan, whose walkway is closed; the Williamsburg; and the Verrazano-Narrows. Running south, toward Bay Ridge, the runner will see the towers of the Verrazano begin to peek over the tops of brownstones about five miles out. And a foot approach to the Verrazano—all the while, one is conscious of one's humble relationship to it—is plain awesome. It can cause the runner to stop in mid-training-stride and wonder how such an effortless-looking span made it across the Narrows, and perhaps to vow to run the New York City Marathon simply for the once-a-year chance to cross this bridge on foot. The Verrazano must be the height of Exalted Running.

In Brooklyn, unlike Queens, Staten Island, and the Bronx, people usually run to where they run, and the real locus of organized Brooklyn running activity is the arrowhead-shaped swath of Prospect Park. The races in Prospect Park have the feel of small-town gatherings—usually they are of such a friendly size, say two hundred or three hundred people, a very old-fashioned and intimate size by Manhattan's mega-race standards. The park has a famous tree, the Camperdown Elm, that nearly died a few years back from simple neglect. Now the citizens of Brooklyn, under the aegis of the Friends of Prospect Park, run to benefit their trees, four times a year. Their entry fees go for professional tree care and planting.

Along Prospect Park's western border lies the community of Park Slope, one of the world's largest brownstone areas, and in the park Brownstone Running has developed. It is not hard to spot the Brownstone Runner moving over the 3.36-mile loop at a sedate Victorian conversational pace, debating the merits of Restoration versus Renovation or trading names of electricians and plumbers. The Brownstone Runner usually wears paint-spattered T-shirts and shoes and exhibits a serious pride of turf which extends to his local running park.

A subspecies of Brownstone Running is the Brooklyn pastime known as "running and antiquing." It consists of a slow run up one side of Atlantic Avenue from Brooklyn Heights to Times Plaza at Atlantic and Flatbush, and a slow run back down the other side, following the route of the annual 2.5-mile Atlantic Antic race, which happens to be the prime antiquing route in Brooklyn as well as the place to find Arab food.

In Brooklyn Heights, a different running syndrome has developed. There, the denizens become so hooked on their promenade and harbor view that they do repeats of the Heights .33-Mile like metronomes and call it running, though the surface is uneven asphalt tile and the pollution from the Brooklyn-Queens Expressway is considerable. The Heights is a nice run for beginners, but many seem never to budge beyond it. One-third of a mile inland, via the Heights' fruit streets—Cranberry, Orange, and Pineapple—is Cadman Plaza Park. Here the full .5-mile track can be run on dirt or concrete sidewalk. The plaza's dirt runners (it's dull but it's dirt) look down on the plaza's concrete runners and both seem to regard the promenade faithful as unenlightened.

In Brooklyn, as elsewhere, cemetery running is not allowed, but Greenwood Cemetery's periphery nonetheless provides one of the great cemetery runs. In fact, Greenwood, encompassing 478 acres and a half million souls, ought to be run. The ultimate in Victorian Gothic Revival funerary statuary sumptuousness is to be seen here, as well as Brooklyn's high point of 216.5 feet.

Though the borough still lacks a Brooklyn Bums Track Club, the Prospect Park T.C. meets Sunday mornings at nine for group runs of near-marathon distance. And the Brooklyn Long Run, the longest of the Borough Long Runs, at 44 miles, begins and ends on the Brooklyn Bridge. It offers the challenge of a marathon and a half, and perhaps ought to be called the Brooklyn Ultra-Long Run.

PROSPECT PARK

3.36 miles inner-drive
3.68 miles sidewalk-perimeter

One of the city's great parks, designed by Frederick Law Olmsted and Calvert Vaux, Prospect creates the pleasant illusion of country running. It provides a mostly gentle 3.36-mile tour through Olmsted and Vaux's second major New York park, considered by some to be their finest. (Park patresfamilias will swear that the distance is a regular 3.5 miles. It is not—just remember the standard deductible when you surprise yourself in Prospect with the fastest 3.5-mile time of your running career.) As recently as 1972, Prospect Park had a hardy core of runners, almost all men and almost all old-timers. Now the age level has dropped, the women are out there, the numbers are up, and since the summer of 1978 the inner track of the three-lane Park Drive has been reserved for runners and bicyclists twenty-four hours a day, year round. (Motorists are generally respectful of the road-sharing scheme.)

Prospect is a smaller, more closely held park than Central, and, like a closely held company, more easily controlled. Park loyalists like Bob Muller, of the Prospect Park Track Club, describe it as "just the right distance. In Prospect you are never too far from home, never more than a mile and a half. And you can do four or five loops and never run the same course." On weekends and holidays (7 P.M. Friday to 6 A.M. Monday) and on summer days (10 A.M. to 3 P.M. and 7 P.M. to 10 P.M.), the park's drives belong to a peaceable kingdom of runners, cyclists, skaters, and walkers. In these hours, the park offers quiet running, except for the disco porters who take their tape decks out for loud walks.

In Prospect Park, the running is low-key, casual, and noncompetitive except when a woman runner happens to pass a man, which usually causes him, no matter how slow he may be, to speed up in a knee-jerk fit of disbelief. (The other standard reaction is to try to slow her down—talk to her or try to pick her up.) Prospect Park lies just east of the large brownstone colony of Park Slope, a hundred years ago referred to as The Gold Coast. Runners glimpse through a tree screen the mansions lining Prospect Park West. And Brownstone Runners, fresh from their labors in The Victorian Restoration, are a common Prospect Park sight in paint-spattered running gear. They are the born-again people who state convincingly that running is their salvation from eternal stripping and spackling.

Prospect Park, especially in the mile of its Long Meadow, a "sweep of grassland extensive enough to make a really permanent impression on the mind," according to Olmsted and Vaux's plan, could be a small New England valley. The run follows the ups and downs of a terminal moraine ridge, part of the Harbor Hill Moraine, which was dropped mid-Brooklyn by the last ice age about seventy-five thousand years ago, between Flatbush

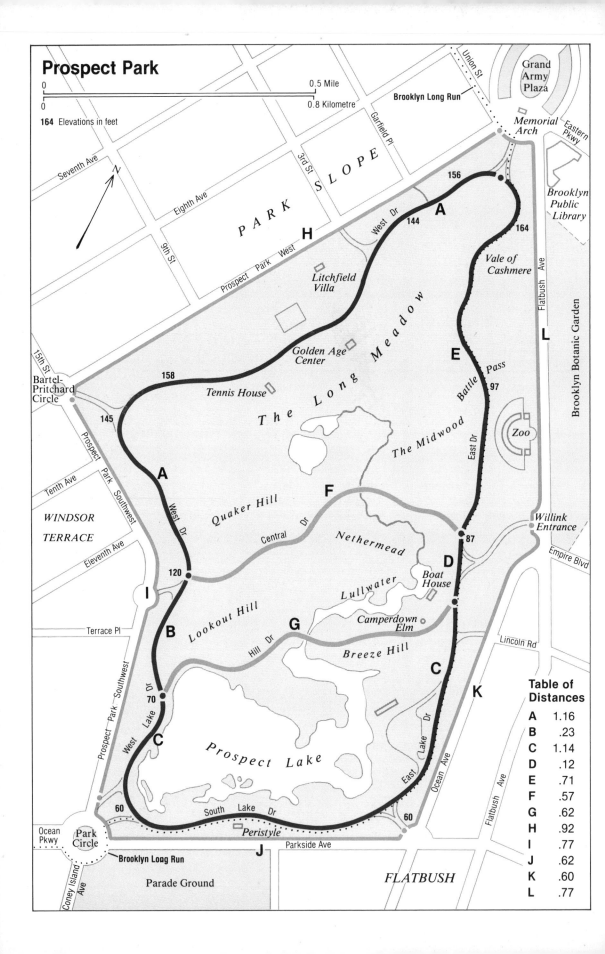

Prospect Park

0   0.5 Mile

0   0.8 Kilometre

164 Elevations in feet

N

PARK SLOPE

Brooklyn Long Run

Union St

Grand Army Plaza

Memorial Arch

Eastern Pkwy

Brooklyn Public Library

Seventh Ave

Eighth Ave

Garfield Pl

3rd St

West Dr

156

144

A

164

Vale of Cashmere

Flatbush Ave

9th St

Prospect Park West

H

Litchfield Villa

Golden Age Center

The Long Meadow

Battle Pass

97

E

L

Brooklyn Botanic Garden

158

Tennis House

The Midwood

East Dr

Zoo

15th St

Bartel-Pritchard Circle

145

A

West Dr

Quaker Hill

Central Dr

F

Nethermead

Willink Entrance

Tenth Ave

WINDSOR TERRACE

Eleventh Ave

120

Lookout Hill

Lullwater

Camperdown Elm

Boat House

87

D

Empire Blvd

I

B

Hill Dr

G

Breeze Hill

Lincoln Rd

Terrace Pl

Prospect Park Southwest

70

C

West Lake Dr

Prospect Lake

East Lake Dr

C

K

Flatbush Ave

60

South Lake Dr

Peristyle

60

Ocean Ave

Ocean Pkwy

Park Circle

Brooklyn Long Run

J

Parkside Ave

FLATBUSH

Coney Island Ave

Parade Ground

Table of Distances

A	1.16
B	.23
C	1.14
D	.12
E	.71
F	.57
G	.62
H	.92
I	.77
J	.62
K	.60
L	.77

Avenue and Prospect Park Southwest. There are enough rolling hills, forests, streams, and lakes in the park—"an agreeable variety of surface and fair prospects both of distant and local scope," according to its makers —to make it seem larger than 526 acres. It may surprise the city runner to find such diversity of landscape in a park of such neat size. The curvaceous Park Drive manages by the deceit of bits, to make the miles pass faster. And there is enough forest here to see the trees. Distinguished hundred-year-old beeches, European horse chestnuts, pin oaks, unblighted elms, Japanese scholar trees, and the exotic Camperdown Elm. The Camperdown, near the Lullwater Pond and the Boat House, is worth a stop-out. (Most runners are oblivious to it, owing to its secluded placement.) Described in *Tree Trails in Prospect Park* as "the most distinguished tree in the city and possibly in the state," it is a variety of prostrate elm from Scotland, from the estate of the Earl of Camperdown, grafted onto the trunk of an upright American elm. It grows like an irregular weeping umbrella and nearly died in the late sixties, at the age of a hundred. The poet Marianne Moore, with the Friends of Prospect Park, raised the money to hire tree surgeons to fill the tree's cavities and cable its heavy horizontal limbs. And now the Friends of Prospect Park hold four Tree Benefit races each year, to provide more tree care and planting in the park.

Prospect offers Operatic and Philharmonic running in summer, when the Metropolitan Opera and the New York Philharmonic hold forth in the Long Meadow, not far from the Park Drive. At the southern end of the park you can usually choose the beat of the drummer you want to run to—African, Caribbean, calypso. Here, the smell of grass usually hangs heavy on the air, though after a summer rain the clover is even stronger.

If you are fond of historical running, Battle Pass in Prospect Park is where George Washington led the Battle of Long Island, kickoff fight of the Revolutionary War in 1776. Battle Pass is *the* hill in Prospect. It should be taken slowly and with respect, but it seems to get easier with acquaintance. To the east of Battle Pass is the Vale of Cashmere, the favorite resting spot in Brooklyn for migrating birds on the spring-fall flyway, which passes directly over the year round runway.

PROSPECT PARK—MEASURED COURSES

2 miles	F + B + C + D	minus .06 mile
3 miles	F + B + C + D + (F x 2)	minus .20 mile
3 miles	F + B + C + G + B	**plus** .21 mile
4 miles	A + B + C + D + (E x 2)	minus .07 mile
5 miles	A + B + C + D + E + A + F	minus .09 mile
5 miles	H + I + J + K + (L x 2) + K	minus .05 mile
6 miles	A + B + C + D + E + A + B + C + D	minus .01 mile
8 miles	(A + B + C + D + E) x 2 + A + B	minus .11 mile
10 miles	(A + B + C + D + E) x 3	minus .08 mile
12 miles	(A + B + C + D + E) x 3 + A + B + G	minus .09 mile

The Sunday morning runs of the Prospect Park Track Club begin promptly at nine from the tennis courts at Park Circle and Parkside Avenue. These outings, up to 24 miles, but often in the 18- to 20-mile range frequently head across the Brooklyn Bridge, up to Central Park and back. Sometimes the route is out to Bay Ridge and Coney Island for a half-portion of the Brooklyn Long Run. The company is good, and the groupings are by speed.

FOOTING: Reasonably smooth, turtlebacked asphalt roadway; comfortable bark-and-sand bridle path that parallels the road much of the way; elsewhere a narrow dirt footpath, irregular in places; one good uphill and downhill each loop; a rugged cross-country course over the grass and ridges; exterior sidewalk of uneven concrete, cracked-up, with much glass.

COURSE DIRECTIONS: Enter the park wherever. Follow the roadway clockwise or counterclockwise; same for sidewalk.

HAZARDS: Unleashed or abandoned dogs; high-speed bicycle racers; one high-speed trotting horse and cart; rogue automobiles that crash through police barricades; pods of teen-agers hanging out on the Prospect Park West and Southwest benches, drinking and smoking and breaking bottles against the park wall; at night, a running partner or large dog is recommended for the sidewalk circuit (women should not run it alone); inner roadway is relatively unpolluted when the park is closed to traffic; bad exhaust pollution on sidewalk route, particularly on Flatbush Avenue and Prospect Park West.

COMFORTS: Rest rooms at the zoo, skating rink, and Golden Age Center; water fountains throughout the park, but most don't work; usually two or three fire hydrants are turned on to a steady drip through the spring and summer.

MASS TRANSPORT: Seventh Avenue I.R.T. to Grand Army Plaza; D, QB, or QJ to Prospect Park or Parkside Avenue; F or GG to Fifteenth Street–Prospect Park. Parking at the Wollman Rink; street parking on park edges.

EXTENSIONS: 1) From Park Circle and Parkside Avenue it is 5.2 miles out Ocean Parkway to the Coney Island Boardwalk Run. 2) From Grand Army Plaza it is 3.1 miles out Union Street and Court to the Brooklyn Bridge.

CONEY ISLAND—SHEEPSHEAD BAY—
SHORE GREENBELT

2.45 miles, Coney Island Boardwalk
9.82 miles (20 miles round trip), Coney Island to Rockaways

If you're a novice on boardwalks, the 2.45-mile Coney Island one ought to be your first—for the feel of the spring in the new boards, for the seedy carnival atmosphere and the fresh-fried salt air. From the beginning of the run, at West Thirty-seventh, fix on the end hurdle—the Marine Parkway Bridge, the lift from Brooklyn to Queens, the Rockaways. The bridge looks effortlessly small at a nine-mile glance. Keep it in mind. It will grow on you.

The special Coney Island ambience, a holdover from the early twentieth century, is part corn-on-the-cob carnival—pink cotton candy, the original Nathan's Famous, fried everything (hope that the distance runner's aversion to food smells doesn't peak here)—and part eastern Europe, maybe Odessa in summer. Elderly eastern Europeans spend sunny afternoons camped on the boardwalk, beach chairs drawn up into gossip-klatsch circles. Coney Island is a run through an antique, perfectly gone-to-seed American summer resort where every day the flag withers over the front doors of beach shacks on stilts. Much Brooklynese, and little English, spoken here.

The 1.8 miles of street-sidewalk running through Brighton Beach (named for the one in England, but Brooklyn's is not the end point of a mythic 52.5-mile race) and Manhattan Beach breaks the seedy Coney Island mood. The streets here are marked with the indelible stigmata of all New York City streets—cracks, potholes, tar patches—but the homes of Manhattan Beach have, otherwise, the neatly landscaped, kept-up look of a New Jersey suburb.

Run over water on the Ocean Avenue Bridge, a footpath over the Sheepshead Bay inlet. Berthed on the other side are fishing launches—fish for smell, fish for sale, and Lundy's for seafood dinner—if not piroshki at one of the new Russian-immigrant shops in the area.

At Knapp Street and the beginning of the dunes path, again pick up the Marine Parkway Bridge by eye. Underfoot is the well-sanded asphalt of the Shore Parkway Greenbelt. Run on the refreshment of sea breeze, unless the wind blows the wrong way, in which case you will choke on auto exhaust. The land lies low here, gives the feel of wide open spaces, seeing afar. Off to the left appears a mini-Manhattan, looking like a paste-up against the sky. Manhattan begins to accompany you as a static point. How did Manhattan ever get so small? Manhattan reduced to a symbolic pseudo-mirage cannot be right, especially when seen topping dune grass and cattails. Things are out of proportion, giving a real sense of distance covered.

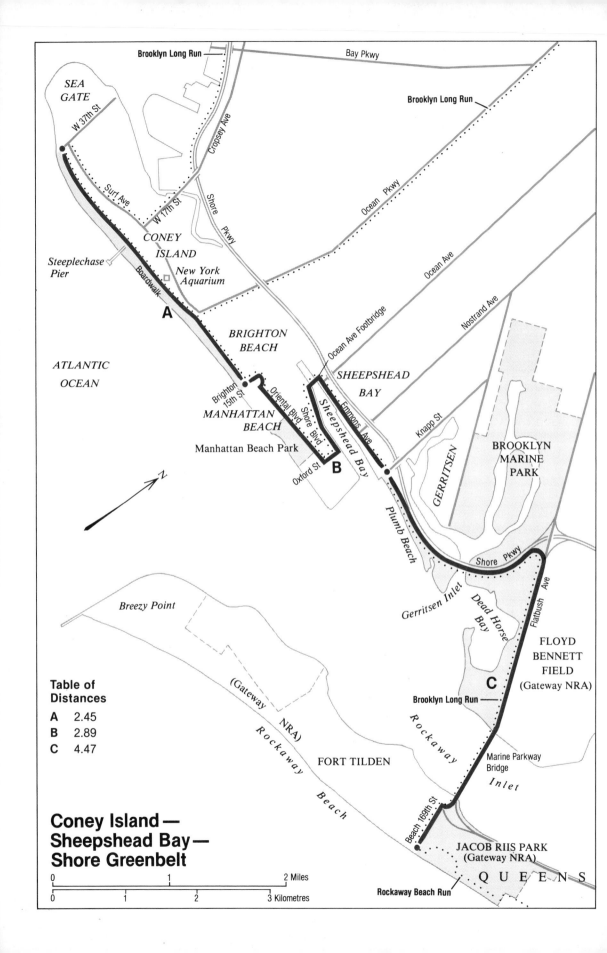

SEA GATE

Brooklyn Long Run

Bay Pkwy

Brooklyn Long Run

W 37th St

Cropsey Ave

Surf Ave

W 17th St

Shore Pkwy

Ocean Pkwy

CONEY ISLAND

Steeplechase Pier

Boardwalk

New York Aquarium

Ocean Ave

A

BRIGHTON BEACH

Ocean Ave Footbridge

SHEEPSHEAD BAY

Nostrand Ave

ATLANTIC OCEAN

Brighton 15th St

Oriental Blvd

Shore Blvd

Sheepshead Bay

Emmons Ave

Knapp St

BROOKLYN MARINE PARK

MANHATTAN BEACH

Manhattan Beach Park

Oxford St

B

GERRITSEN

N

Plumb Beach

Shore Pkwy

FLOYD BENNETT FIELD (Gateway NRA)

Breezy Point

Gerritsen Inlet

Dead Horse Bay

Flatbush Ave

C

Table of Distances

A   2.45
B   2.89
C   4.47

(Gateway NRA)

Rockaway Beach

Rockaway

Brooklyn Long Run

FORT TILDEN

Inlet

Marine Parkway Bridge

Beach 169th St

Coney Island — Sheepshead Bay — Shore Greenbelt

JACOB RIIS PARK (Gateway NRA)

QUEENS

0   1   2 Miles

0   1   2   3 Kilometres

Rockaway Beach Run

This is a flat relaxed course, except for the push needed to put you over the top of the Marine Parkway Bridge. The only element this run lacks is fire, but the earth, the air, and the water smell fresh as Nantucket, make it seem like a 20-mile afternoon vacation from the city.

FOOTING: Fresh boardwalk at Coney Island, recently restored; flat asphalt street or concrete sidewalk to and around Sheepshead Bay; sanded asphalt path from Knapp Street to Rockaways. Flat except for two small bridges and a large one. A few low spots between Knapp Street and the Marine Parkway Bridge, where dune erosion obliterates the path under a depth of sand; just before Flatbush Avenue rain-filled marsh mud puddles may swamp the path; fine night running on the boardwalk; the distance is considered safe for lone women runners in daylight, unsafe at night.

COURSE DIRECTIONS: Pick up the Coney Island Boardwalk beyond Surf on West Thirty-seventh and head east; go left at Brightwater and Fifteenth (A); right onto Brighton Beach; left onto Oxford Street; left on Shore Boulevard; right on Ocean Avenue Bridge; right on Emmons; straight on sidewalk to juncture of Knapp and Shore Parkway (B); continue straight on asphalt path between dunes and Shore Parkway; path crosses small bridge opposite Gerritsen, curves right before a big traffic circle, and runs along right side of Flatbush Avenue to and over the Marine Parkway Bridge; cross left onto Beach 169th and head straight out to the Rockaway sand in Jacob Riis Park (C). Retrace to return.

HAZARDS: Occasional nailheads sticking up on boardwalk; bicycles; on sunny afternoons, weekends, and holidays, boardwalk crowds make for stop-and-go dodg'em running (best to run early or late); broken bottles; buses and cars where streets are crossed or shared with traffic; exhaust pollution if Shore Parkway is without breeze; chill winter winds along the boardwalk and on the Marine Parkway Bridge.

COMFORTS: Water fountains that work, along boardwalk and Shore Parkway Greenbelt; rest rooms at New York Aquarium and off boardwalk and at Jacob Riis Park, in the Rockaways.

MASS TRANSPORT: I.N.D. D, F, or B train, B.M.T. M, N, or QB train to Coney Island and Stillwell Avenue to start at west end of Coney Island Boardwalk; D, M or QB train to Sheepshead Bay (this works to shortcut the return trip). Street parking available.

EXTENSIONS: 1) 5.2 miles on Ocean Parkway from Coney Island to Prospect Park. 2) 2.74 miles from the boardwalk and West Thirty-seventh to Bensonhurst and the Bay Ridge Run.

BROOKLYN MINI-RUNS

BROOKLYN HEIGHTS PROMENADE: The .33-mile Heights Promenade is quite possibly the most heavily run fraction of a mile in Brooklyn. Though the asphalt-tile surface is somewhat uneven and hard on the bones—and the exhaust fumes rising from the Brooklyn-Queens Expressway, which is tucked beneath the cantilevered esplanade are less than healthful—the wide-angle harbor view, the lower Manhattan profile, the cobwire-webbing of the Brooklyn Bridge, and the charm of the brownstone town houses fronting the promenade make this run rich. There is too much to see, and the harbor composition changes constantly, as freighters berth at your feet, ferries ply, tugs chug. No comforts here, but several fountains. Safe by day and by night. Though the basic run is short, it has good connections. From the north end, where the Jehovah's Witnesses headquarters stands, turn right onto Middagh (at Columbia Heights) for the .33-mile run to Cadman Plaza. At Cadman Plaza, there is a pleasant, shady park for a .5-mile loop. Exit onto Cadman Plaza East, run downhill and left to pick up the stairs to the Brooklyn Bridge for the mile run across to Manhattan. (Or spend an hour running against traffic on the one-way lanes of the Heights to capture for yourself the look of an aristocratic nineteenth-century American community.) Handiest subway: I.R.T. Seventh Avenue express to Clark Street and run four blocks to the promenade.

FORT GREENE PARK: Fort Greene Park sits on a hundred-foot-high hill bounded on the north and east by elegant brownstones in intermediate stages of decline or epiphany, and on the south and west by public housing projects. The park was an 1860 creation of Frederick Law Olmsted and Calvert Vaux, while the Prison Ship Martyr's Monument (to the ten thousand prisoners in the Revolutionary War who died in British ships nearby) was added in 1908 by Stanford White. The outer park trail, .84 mile of comfortable asphalt, can be picked up on Myrtle, Cumberland, or DeKalb Avenue, and followed along the park's perimeter until it climbs to the hill monument. On top, there is shade, water, an excellent view across to Manhattan, and a classical comfort station—a Doric temple. The park has good gradations of hillwork up to a hundred feet from around twenty. Fairly safe by day, though women should never run alone here. No safe night running. Overall, a rough area. Handiest subway stop: DeKalb Avenue on the D, B, M, N, QB, or RR train and a five-block walk east on DeKalb.

GREENWOOD CEMETERY: For excessively Romantique moods, the 3.5-mile run around Greenwood Cemetery has the statuary. Running the 20 miles of pathway inside the fence is not allowed, but the on-runner can see a great deal of ornate stonework, especially in the guardian-angel line, from the circumference. Part of the Romantic Movement in landscape architecture, Greenwood makes for a Romantic run, despite the choices of surface: concrete sidewalk littered with broken bottles; edge of corrugated asphalt road—the McDonald Avenue stretch being a truck route and leaving plenty of diesel *sur l'air.* Whether running the road or the sidewalk, be on the lookout for potholes. The run takes you around, but not over, Brooklyn's highest point of 216.5 feet. Since 1840, more than half a million people have been buried in Greenwood. As you run you might think of Currier & Ives, Samuel F. B. Morse, Boss Tweed, Lola Montez, the Reverend Henry Ward Beecher, Horace Greeley, DeWitt Clinton—all here. The Gothic Revival gatehouse at Fifth Avenue and Twenty-fifth is a wild confection. To get there, take the B.M.T. B, N, or RR train to Thirty-sixth Street or run the nine blocks south from Prospect Park.

SUNSET PARK: The perimeter of this modest bluff park measures .84 mile on the concrete sidewalk. The park is set between Fifth and Seventh Avenues, and Forty-first and Forty-fourth Streets, with a block-long hill workout as part of either Forty-first or Forty-fourth. There are fine harbor views from the top of the park. The neighborhood, once predominantly Scandinavian, is now a Scandinavian-Hispanic mix. Nearest subways: B train to Ninth Avenue, or RR train to Forty-fifth Street.

OWL'S HEAD PARK: Owl's Head Park is small but lovely. Almost the entire park is a hill, planted in trees. The impression is of the sweep of a hundred-foot-high hill. The reward, at the summit, is a panoramic view of New York Harbor and the shipping lanes, as one ignores the neglect and ruin of the hilltop promenade, where teen-age revelers have broken their bottles for years. Owl's Head is a good warmup for the Bay Ridge Run to Bensonhurst, with smooth asphalt path all the way, except for a portion of asphalt tile on the hilltop. Much of the distance can be run on grass, and the inner .5-mile loop is excellent for hillwork. Chief hazards are children on bicycles and Big Wheels—and does this path ever have glass! There are no comforts, and the fountains are broken.

At Sixty-seventh Street and Colonial Road, take the asphalt path to the right that loops around the outer edge of the park. Follow it (Shore Parkway is to your right, then Sixty-eighth Street) until asphalt ends at Colonial Road; go left on well-trod dirt path that passes the basketball courts for .83 mile. Beginning at the same spot take the inner asphalt path that heads up and around the hill. Follow it left across the brow (pausing to take in the view). Drop down, loop left, and return to the start for a cumulative 1.31 miles. From Sixty-eighth and Shore Road walk one block south to the Sixty-ninth Street pier and the beginning of the Bay Ridge Run.

GERRITSEN CREEK TRAIL: A 1.5-mile run on a firmly packed sand road that winds through the marsh of the Gerritsen Creek basin, part of the developing—or as yet undeveloped, depending on how you see it—Brooklyn Marine Park, east of Sheepshead Bay. The course is flat but rutted, without shade, and usually breezy. Expect encounters with wading shore birds, dead rusted cars, sweet sea air.

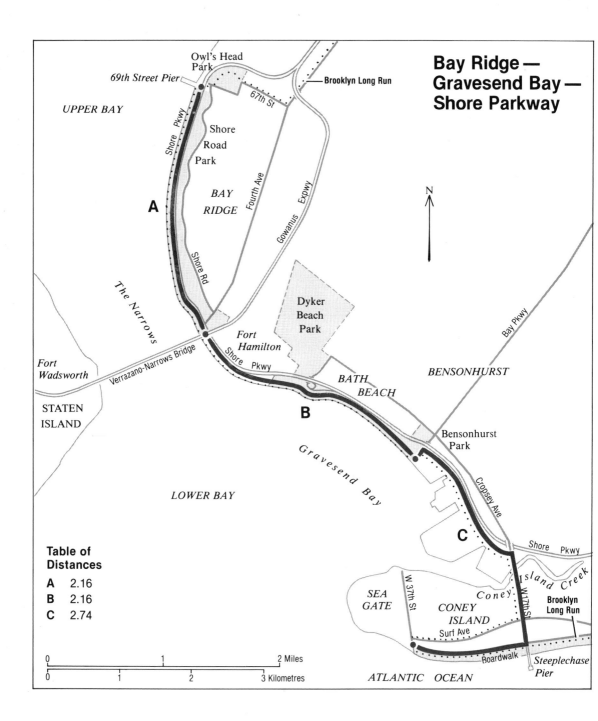

Bay Ridge —
Gravesend Bay —
Shore Parkway

Owl's Head Park

69th Street Pier

Brooklyn Long Run

67th St

UPPER BAY

Shore Pkwy

Shore Road Park

Fourth Ave

Gowanus Expwy

BAY RIDGE

A

N

Shore Rd

The Narrows

Dyker Beach Park

Fort Hamilton

Shore Pkwy

Fort Wadsworth

Verrazano-Narrows Bridge

BATH BEACH

BENSONHURST

STATEN ISLAND

B

Bensonhurst Park

LOWER BAY

Gravesend Bay

Cropsey Ave

C

Shore Pkwy

Table of Distances

A	2.16
B	2.16
C	2.74

Island Creek

SEA GATE

W 37th St

Coney

W 17th St

Brooklyn Long Run

CONEY ISLAND

Surf Ave

Steeplechase Pier

Boardwalk

ATLANTIC OCEAN

0	1	2 Miles
0	1	2	3 Kilometres

BAY RIDGE—GRAVESEND BAY—SHORE PARKWAY

4.32 miles

Part of the 44-mile Brooklyn Long Run, this great curve of a course passes *under* Mile 2 of the New York City Marathon. If the urge to run the Verrazano is ever to hit you, here is where it will happen, as you are overwhelmed by a feeling of insignificance up close to this bridge. (And the only way to gain pedestrian rights to the bridge is to run the New York City Marathon.) If it were not for the sweeping views of the Upper Bay, The Narrows, the Verrazano-Narrows Bridge, and Gravesend Bay, this would be a most unprepossessing run. The course, over a thin strip of asphalt misnamed Shore Road Park—one of Robert Moses' afterthoughts while belting the Brooklyn waterfront with the Shore Parkway—is saved by the scenery: archetypal views of a greatly reduced Manhattan, The Lady, Staten Island, the entire harbor. The Parkway offers cheek-by-chassis running at its most intimate, on a path almost barren of trees or shade and, lacking a good breeze off the water, in profoundly auto-polluted air. Furthermore, the objective at the Bensonhurst end turns out to be a seaside shopping mall of grand proportion, with an asphalt pasture and a luminous white building as beacon—Korvette's. This is a heavily trafficked run-way, home turf for Bay Ridge and Bensonhurst runners. Best seasons are spring and fall, early morning and evening in summer; chilling in winter. The Bay Ridge area, once famous for being Scandinavian, is now famous for the movie *Saturday Night Fever* which was filmed here.

FOOTING: Asphalt pavement about fifteen feet wide; so badly eroded in many places along the sea wall near the Verrazano Bridge that the bulkhead stones and guardrail have dropped into The Narrows (these holes are fenced off); absolutely flat surface; occasional stretches of dirt path beside the asphalt.

COURSE DIRECTIONS: From Bay Ridge, begin at Shore Road and the Sixty-ninth Street pier; from Bensonhurst, begin at Shore Parkway and Bay Parkway. Either way, follow the shoreline.

OTHER RUNS: Some runners choose the inland strip on the other side of the Shore Parkway, for dirt and grass surfaces on the 2.2 miles between the Sixty-ninth Street pier and the Verrazano, but waterside down is *it.*

HAZARDS: Dogs and bicycles on the loose; big sea holes and pavement crackup by guard rail; absence of guardrail; sunburn and wind exposure.

COMFORTS: Broken water fountains en route; rest rooms at the Bensonhurst shopping mall; some picnic spots.

MASS TRANSPORT: B.M.T. RR train to Bay Ridge Avenue for the Sixty-ninth Street pier start; RR to Bay Parkway at Eighty-sixth Street for the Bensonhurst end. Street parking available.

EXTENSION: From Bensonhurst, there is a 2.74-mile run to the Coney Island Boardwalk.

BROOKLYN MINI-RUNS

HIGHLAND PARK: Highland Park straddles the Brooklyn-Queens border, its Brooklyn section being a steep hill rising from Jamaica Avenue to the Ridgewood Reservoir in Queens. It offers good resistance work on either the .46-mile loop of the ball fields or the .40-mile concrete sidewalk of the Park Drive dogleg (known locally as Snake Hill), and around to the steps up to the reservoir.

Though few runners appear to have made the climb up the glass-garlanded route to the reservoir, its 1.2-mile asphalt loop featuring fresh breezes off the water would seem to be the choice local spot for top running.

Working fountains along Vermont Place in the Park. QJ train to Cleveland Street, three blocks from the park.

BROWER PARK: There are three circuits possible in this Crown Heights park: a run of the park perimeter on concrete for .5 mile; a circuit of the inner asphalt path beginning at the stairs up from St. Marks Avenue at Brooklyn Avenue to the B.C.M. (you will learn that the large freeway-style B.C.M. sign over the park means Brooklyn Children's Museum, which is buried in the hill in Brower Park and has been in the vicinity since 1899) for .33 mile; and a .15-mile circuit of the fenced oval of grass at the south off-center of this park. Combining the three routes gives a variety of surfaces, a small steep hill, a long flight of stairs, and several gentle grades. The outer loop, however, has the architecture. The brownstones and mansions along St. Mark's Avenue are handsome enough to stop you mid-run, in awe of the beauty of some of the finest houses in New York City. There are fountains and fire hydrants for water. Used by neighborhood runners. Take the I.R.T. No. 2 to Kingston Avenue at Eastern Parkway. (Be careful; muggings along Eastern Parkway are frequent.)

LINCOLN TERRACE PARK: This park remains unmeasured. As Patti Hagan was taking the first bike-calibrator reading on Eastern Parkway, she was assaulted and thrown off her bicycle by two young Crown Heights men, who made off with the bike after threatening to shoot her. Soon thereafter, the police informed her that pimps, prostitutes, muggers, and smack dealers run Lincoln Terrace Park—nobody else. Stay away.

McCARREN PARK: McCarren is Greenpoint's identifiably W.P.A. (1936) park, with facilities for something of everything—an enormous swimming pool, a .25-mile cinder track, baseball diamonds, basketball courts, tennis courts—within a 1.22-mile sidewalk perimeter. The park has the shape of an abstract arrow, and though that 1.22 miles constitutes McCarren's longest run, it is not necessarily the preferred run, as there are about seven streets to cross. The quality of the perimeter footing varies from glass-encrusted concrete to glass-encrusted asphalt tile. Many runners here like the .65-mile Bedford Avenue–Driggs Avenue–North Twelfth Street loop because of the shade trees along it. The other favored loop is on the .25-mile cinder track, though on cloudless days the sun is glaring here. There are water fountains and leaky hydrants for water stops. Greenpoint remains a sturdy eastern European community within the city. On the North Twelfth Street side of the run, you pass the Russian Orthodox Cathedral of the Transfiguration—five onion domes. And there is an absolutely transfixing broadside profile of midtown Manhattan when you look west from Bedford Avenue—which is also Mile 12 of the New York City Marathon. Nearby are a number of streets, such as Dobbin Street, on which you can manage a .33- or .50-mile run on the straightaway. LL or GG train to Nassau and Manhattan Avenues.

McGOLDRICK PARK: Though only .5 mile around on the outer sidewalk, this small green a few blocks northeast of McCarren has many lofty shade trees and much dignity. It is as quiet, clean, and tidy as any Warsaw street, and this park has not been abandoned to youth—elderly people klatsch here and whole families spend their summer evenings seated either on the park's many (unvandalized) benches or on lawn chairs brought from home. The outer sidewalk is concrete, with tufted grass. The inner, .4-mile asphalt path is flat, smooth, and easy to navigate. The languages overheard here sound the way the Cyrillic alphabet looks—exotic and incomprehensible. The scale of this dorp is small, human, unpretentious; and the flower gardens in surrounding yards are obviously well loved. The water fountains work.

On nearby streets, *mitteleuropean*-style, people sit on their stoops in the evening, or on chairs on the sidewalk in front of their homes, and visit. Women chat while leaning out windows, arms comfortably bedded on window pillows. You may feel you are running through a solid community, one in Poland perhaps—one of Isaac Singer's *shtetls*, almost. The "American Grocery" on the corner of Humboldt Street and Enger Avenue seems entirely appropriate. This park has charm on the half shell. There is a statue commemorating the battle of the Monitor and the Merrimac. In January 1862, the Monitor, which had been built in Greenpoint, was launched here—as was Mae West, somewhat later. LL or GG train to Nassau and Manhattan Avenues.

TOMPKINS PARK: A small Bedford-Stuyvesant park frequented by neighborhood runners, who do the .48-mile outer-sidewalk loop under large old shade trees. The park is the heart of a once-elegant brownstone square à la Bloomsbury. Some of the houses have been burned and vandalized, but others are holding their own. On the Lafayette Avenue side, in front of a wrecked brownstone, grows an antique (hundred-year-old) southern tree of note, the Magnolia Grandiflora. Originally designed by Olmsted and Vaux. GG to Myrtle–Willoughby Avenue–Marcy Avenue.

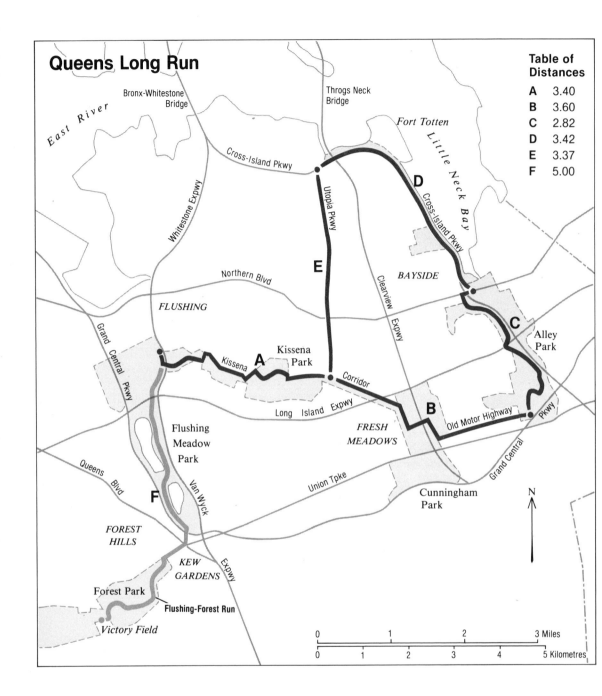

Queens Long Run

Table of Distances

A	3.40
B	3.60
C	2.82
D	3.42
E	3.37
F	5.00

East River

Bronx-Whitestone Bridge

Throgs Neck Bridge

Fort Totten

Cross-Island Pkwy

Little Neck Bay

Whitestone Expwy

Utopia Pkwy

D

Cross-Island Pkwy

Northern Blvd

E

BAYSIDE

Clearview Expwy

FLUSHING

Grand Central Pkwy

Kissena

A

Kissena Park

C

Alley Park

Corridor

Long Island Expwy

B

Old Motor Highway

Pkwy

Grand Central

Flushing Meadow Park

FRESH MEADOWS

Queens Blvd

Van Wyck

F

Union Tpke

Cunningham Park

N

FOREST HILLS

KEW GARDENS

Expwy

Forest Park

Flushing-Forest Run

Victory Field

0		1		2		3 Miles
0	1	2	3	4		5 Kilometres

QUEENS

Nobody comes from Queens and nobody runs there. If you were to canvass that borough, you would find people who run Flushing, Astoria, Forest, Kissena, Cunningham, Bayside, Douglaston, College Point, and Alley—but nobody who runs Queens. Queens is an amalgam of small-town parts. Queens runners are—as are Queens citizens—fiercely loyal to their townish wapentakes. Queens isn't known for running, the way it is for Archie Bunker and for tennis, though it has hundreds of runners and many excellent runner habitats.

If the most you have ever noted about Queens is its acres of cemeteries en route to Kennedy airport, the variety of runscapes there will most likely surprise and please. Queens offers the Rockaway Boardwalk for beach-side running, Little Neck Bay for Bayside running, Astoria Park for riverside and authentic Greek running, and many small lakes for lake circling. Go to Alley or Cunningham or Forest Park for woods runs. Try Baisley Pond if you must run near a major airport. Run Kissena for small charms and Flushing Meadow for the feel of several retired World's Fairs. Jog Douglaston Manor for the Gatsby look and Jamaica for a dynamic meditative running consciousness, a Sri Chinmoy high.

Queens bears the road-marks and park-marks of Robert Moses, America's mega-road-builder, more strikingly than any other borough, except perhaps the Bronx. The idea for the Kissena Corridor Park—the idea that a green girdle could string Flushing Meadow, Kissena, Cunningham, and Alley Parks together as far as the city line—was his. By building the longest continuous park linkwork in the five boroughs, Robert Moses is solely responsible for the 20-mile Queens Long Run, whereby the runner proceeds on an almost unbroken—if at times tenuously thin—green belt from Flushing Meadow Park, through the Kissena Corridor and Park, through Cunningham Park along Commodore Vanderbilt's Old Motor Highway, through Alley Park beside the Cross-Island Parkway (another Moses creation), and along Little Neck Bay past the Throgs Neck Bridge (his as well). Yet, because of Moses, the major parks of Queens are so thoroughly bound up with parkways and expressways, and so cut up by them, that it is difficult for Queens runners to simply cross a street to their favorite running spot. Instead, they tend to drive to where they run, making theirs the most suburban running in the city.

One outstanding characteristic of Queens running is that it offers almost no resistance. It is hard to find a real hill in Queens—the Ridgewood Reservoir, on the Brooklyn border, sits on a hill and shares it with Brooklyn, but runners to the east must cross into Nassau County for hills. In this borough, bridges such as the Pulaski, the Triborough, the Queensboro, and the Marine Parkway are your best chance to find altitude. One Queens oddity is that Forest Park, with a course just four miles long—and that a rather tortured-looking asymmetrical butterfly—is the hangout for a number of the city's ultra-marathoners of 40-mile to 100km strength, and it is the staging area for two competitions at those distances. (Allan Kirik, the A.A.U. American record holder at 50 miles, regularly prowls the north-south, east-west axes of Queens in pursuit of his daily mileage dose.) Flushing Meadow Park is an active race center, especially for families, under the aegis of the Flushing Meadow Track Club. Flushing Meadow has this country's only A.A.U.-certified 100-mile course and holds one competition at that distance each year—44 times around the 2.27-mile Meadow Lake. Instead of suffering circular boredom, given the Catch-22 nature of their task, the ultras love it. It is *efficient,* and the aid station recurs every 2.27 miles. A lot of age-group activity for youngsters goes on in Alley Park.

Though Queens is the largest of the five boroughs, the New York City Marathon treads barely a mile there, and much of the Queens Mile is on the bridges. Still, in Long Island City, the marathon passes through a Little Italy for a stretch, then through a Hispanic area. And in 1978 an institution with headquarters in Jamaica, Queens—perhaps the city's leading spiritual-running center—claimed more entrants in the New York City Marathon than did any running club. It was the Sri Chinmoy Center, one of a string of meditation centers operated by an Indian guru of that name who recommends running to his disciples as a "dynamic" path to spiritual progress, and who also sponsors road races. Sri Chinmoy believes in combining meditation and athletics and he suggests that people run "in a meditative consciousness." Somewhat in the manner of Dr. George Sheehan, whose favored concept is "running and being," Sri Chinmoy has written "Run and become. Become and run." He has written thousands of devotional songs—among them "O Marathon Runner," in which the marathoner can "in the captain's cosmic oneness play." He says that "spiritual people should practice competitive sports to keep the body fit and to develop dynamism." After a Sri Chinmoy woman was the last finisher recorded in the 1978 edition of the New York City Marathon—seven hours and fifteen minutes—one of her colleagues explained it to a *New Yorker* Talk of the Town reporter: "We're just regular people totally inspired to transcend ourselves. The marathon is all done in a meditative consciousness. We are not necessarily trained in marathon running. We try to develop the spiritual aspiration to do these things. *That* gives us the power to run. Most people think it's just training, but you also need inner running."

Queens yields a great deal to the foot explorer—the surprise that New York City could be so suburban, so small-town, so un New York, and have so many people living in single-story detached houses with white picket fences and rose gardens in areas called Rosedale and Bellerose. And then there's the name. Queens was in fact named for one queen, Catherine of Braganza, Queen to Charles II. You might meditate upon that bit of trivia while you run her democratic plural title-sake. And Queens wears those other exotic names that don't really seem quite to fit—Ozone Park, Utopia, Jamaica—a fact you might ponder between intervals of inner running.

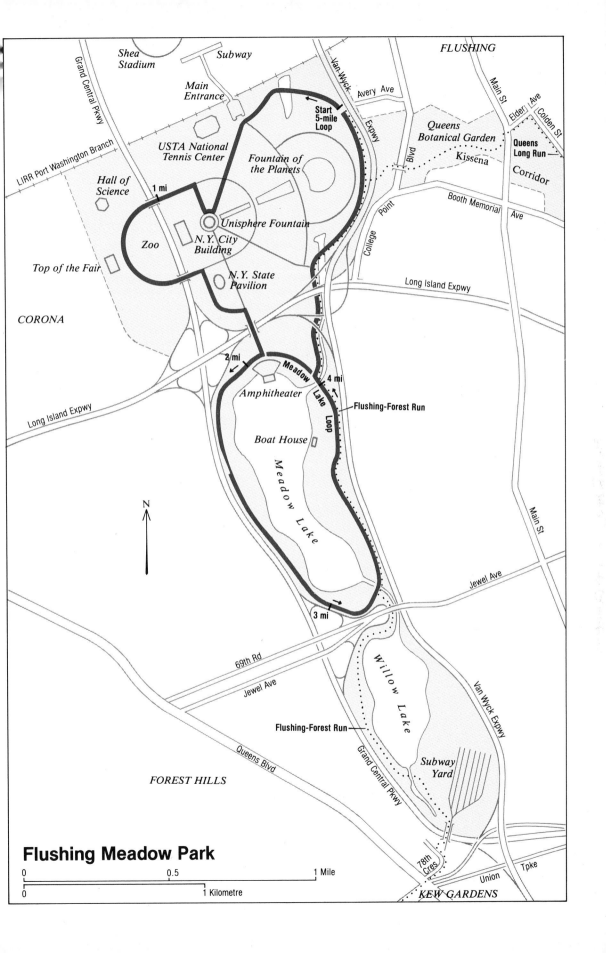

Flushing Meadow Park

0   0.5   1 Mile

0   1 Kilometre

FLUSHING MEADOW PARK

5 miles

Flushing Meadow Park provides the legions of runners who live in Flushing, Corona, Elmhurst, Jackson Heights, etc. with flat road loops around the monumental relics of the 1964-65 World's Fair—the Unisphere, the Fountain of the Planets, the United States and New York Pavilions, a missile, an Astral Fountain, a time capsule—a run through leftover future shock. And there is Meadow Lake, a pleasantly dull body of water-with-breeze, to circle. In this park you have the peculiar feeling that you are running around the Big American Parking Lot, so great is the consideration given to car parking. Turbulent rivers of traffic flow around the park on the Van Wyck and Long Island Expressways and on the Grand Central Parkway. Overhead is near-continuous jet roar, courtesy of J.F.K. and LaGuardia airports. For serene and quietly parkful running, this is the wrong place. Still, Flushing Meadow Park is a very popular running oasis—albeit well paved and manicured almost to sterility—for runners who live nearby. These enthusiastic and friendly folks meet for group runs every Sunday, 9:00 A.M., at the Taystee Bread parking lot off Avery Avenue. Sunday excursions frequently extend south and west to Forest Park and even unto the Brooklyn border at the Ridgewood Reservoir. It's worth a Sunday pilgrimage, or a venturing forth for a Flushing Meadow Park race, of which there are many, under the inspiration of the Flushing Meadow Track Club, to encourage racing and fitness running at all levels. The club's conscientious statistician and course designer, Ben Grundstein, has measured the 2.27 miles around Meadow Lake to the satisfaction of the A.A.U. Long Distance Running Committee, to devise (2.27 miles × 44) the A.A.U.-approved Flushing Meadow 100-mile race course.

FOOTING: Smooth asphalt paths and roadways with a painted green stripe for guidance; flat footing except for a few slight bridge bumps on the Ped Xings over the Grand Central Parkway or the Long Island Expressway.

COURSE DIRECTIONS: Starting at the Avery Avenue entrance to the park, near the Taystee Bread time-and-temp. sign, follow the green stripe.

HAZARDS: Rapists; safe running day and night only if women have partners (at least two women were raped here on summer afternoons in 1978); well lighted at night; only occasional cars; course can be flooded after heavy rain; little shade; fairly constant air and ear pollution since Flushing Meadow is defined by freeways on land and by jet paths in the air.

COMFORTS: Rest rooms in Boat House and tennis house and elsewhere in park; many water fountains that work.

MASS TRANSPORT: I.R.T. No. 7 Flushing Line to Main Street. Walk or run a half mile to the Avery Avenue entrance.

ALLEY PARK

1.9 miles, 1.5 miles, 3 miles, 3.36 miles

Alley Park is a five-hundred-acre sanctified woodland which includes a twenty-three-acre bird sanctuary (pheasants, scarlet tanagers, woodpeckers, quail), ideal for the runner who birds, or the birder who runs. At present, the park has more birders than runners, but the many age-group programs for very young runners held here may tip the balance before too long.

The Alley Park runner has a great choice of trails—north, south, and west—as well as of surface. Whether dirt or asphalt, most of the trails pass through unkempt woods so deep that the trees seem to absorb the sounds of expressway traffic that buffet the park. (Tennis courts and ball fields have invaded Alley only superficially at a couple of perimeter points.)

The park's wild 3-mile North Run gives one of the best cross-country workouts in the city. Among the challenges are the way (finding it and keeping to it), erosion that drops hunks of the trail into gully washouts after heavy rains; low-lying sections that must be forded with care after rain, and the fact that the north section turns into a steaming jungle in summer with a luxuriant overgrowth of brambles and poison ivy that reaches out to grab at you.

The favored, tamest, and most straightforward run in Alley is the 1.9-mile Old Motor Highway west to Cunningham Park. The Old Motor Highway is a fragrant run past the blooming back yards of well-tended Queens on a road unrelated to other roads, a country lane overarched with trees. Commodore Vanderbilt built the road for automobile racing. Here's a pleasant about-foot: a road has been reclaimed from cars for feet.

In southern Alley, the Barbieri Memorial Loops of 1.5 and 3 miles offer wood-and-field running in the park's most populous quadrant. The Barbieri loops were recently laid out on the asphalt paths in white arrows by Ed Quinlan, N.Y.R.R.C. Age Group Race Director, in memory of Donald Barbieri, a longtime running enthusiast from the area.

FOOTING: Mostly smooth asphalt paths, occasional deteriorated patches; choice of dirt or grass surface in some areas. Alley occupies a terminal moraine, which provides gentle inclines (not quite hills) up and down; nice variety of topography on the North Run, with large stones, gully washouts, eroded inclines, tree roots, and fallen trees to contend with.

COURSE DIRECTIONS: 1) Old Motor Highway: Starting at the north end of the Tennis House parking lot off Winchester Boulevard, head west around and behind the tennis courts; go right onto the Old Motor Highway, a wide paved road with distance markers alongside, left over from the Commodore's days. Continue straight until forced to turn back by the chain link fence that is supposed to keep people from crossing the Clear-

67

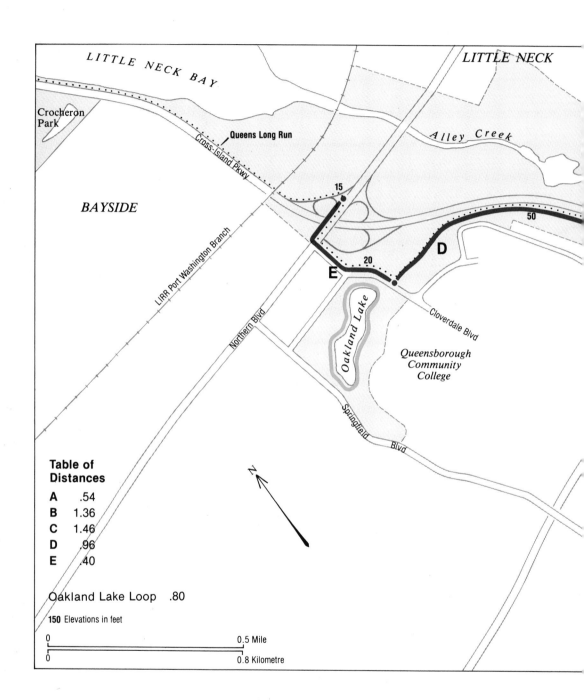

LITTLE NECK BAY

LITTLE NECK

Crocheron Park

Queens Long Run

Alley Creek

Cross-Island Pkwy

BAYSIDE

15

50

LIRR Port Washington Branch

20

D

E

Cloverdale Blvd

Northern Blvd

Oakland Lake

Queensborough Community College

Springfield Blvd

N

Table of Distances

A	.54
B	1.36
C	1.46
D	.96
E	.40

Oakland Lake Loop   .80

150 Elevations in feet

0	0.5 Mile
0	0.8 Kilometre

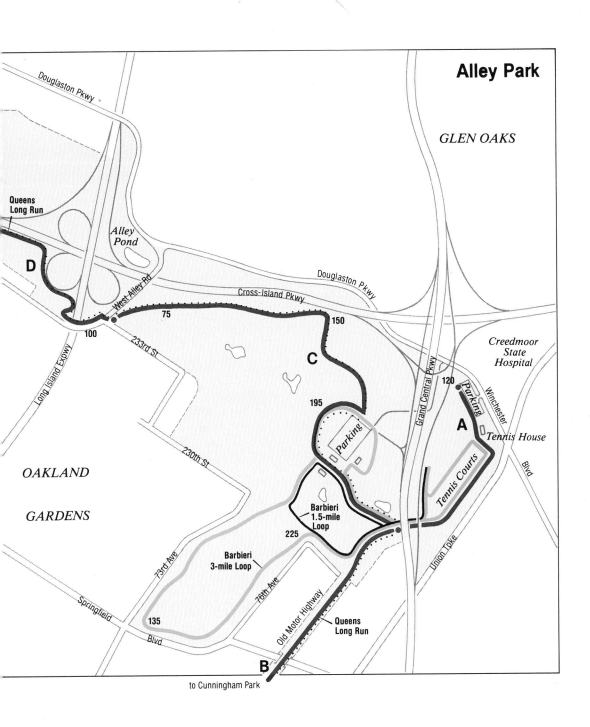

69

view Expressway; or, shortly before the fence, fork right onto a dirt path that leads to Hollis Court Boulevard (A + B). 2) **Barbieri Memorial Loops:** Start and finish for both courses is rather obscure to the uninitiated—it's on the cowpath along the north edge of the field fronting the Tennis House. The starting point is at a maple tree, trunk painted white. Plain white arrows on the asphalt path indicate the 1.5-mile course; crossed white arrows, the 3-mile loop. Both courses begin on the cowpath; head west, parallel to the Grand Central Parkway, on a berm above you; go right on the Old Motor Highway, underpassing the Grand Central; go right at top of hill, on dirt path above Little Alley Pond, then left on asphalt path after a few yards; path skirts the western perimeter of the park. At obvious picnic area (grass, tables) bear left; turn right onto parking-lot sidewalk, right again at end of parking lot; skirt baseball field; go left up hill that climbs into a birch forest; jog slightly left and then straight to the main park-office parking lot; go right on asphalt path leading to steps by Little Alley Pond; left onto Old Motor Highway and left onto the cowpath for 1.5 miles at the maple tree. Follow the hatched arrows for the 3-mile course. 3) **Alley North Run:** Head west on asphalt path from the Tennis House flagpole; right onto the Old Motor Highway (A); right on dirt path and down steps beside Little Alley Pond; straight past park-office parking lot and up hill on asphalt path that curves right above the parking lot; a hundred feet before path enters the parking lot, take dirt path to left around the side of a small rise; after crossing a small stream, head right; path soon becomes asphalt, and it forks; take the left fork north; trail begins to parallel the bridle path; at some places you will be conscious (you can hear it and, in winter, see it) of the Cross-Island Parkway, to your right; follow path over gullies and left, uphill; bear right at hilltop; emerge at the corner of 233rd Street and West Alley (C); cross West Alley and take the stairs to right by a Cross-Island cloverleaf; pick up the asphalt path, left, north for another mile to exit on Cloverdale Boulevard (D).

HAZARDS: Unleashed dogs; teen-agers on power trips (mopeds and motorcycles on Old Motor Highway); truants subbing as muggers; much of the park is wooded, and the running paths isolated (best run with someone, especially recommended for women runners); no night running.

COMFORTS: Rest rooms at park office and Tennis House; cold-water showers for men and women at Tennis House and lockers; drinking fountains along the Barbieri loops.

MASS TRANSPORT: I.R.T. No. 7 to Main Street, then Q12 bus; I.N.D. E or F to Union Turnpike, then Q44A bus; I.N.D. E or F to 179th Street, then Q43 or Q75 bus; E (rush hours only) or F to 169th Street, then Q17A bus; B.M.T. J train to 168th Street, then Q17A bus; parking lots at park headquarters and at Tennis House off Winchester Boulevard.

EXTENSIONS: 1) **Douglaston:** North of Oakland Lake at the north tip of

Alley turn right onto Northern Boulevard; around 235th begin working your way left to Bayshore Boulevard West, which curves east to become Bayshore Boulevard East. The 1.1-mile Douglaston Manor Run begins at Bayshore and 36th Avenue. Turn around at Douglas Road and Grosvenor Street and retrace. This is Great Gatsby country, Bayshore skirting the vast lawns of houses grand and fanciful—slate roofs, gables, gazebos—with views of yachts on Long Island Sound. The course is fairly flat, somewhat potholed; there is little traffic, much shade, only a few tethered dogs, and the air is clean and salty. A delight. 2) **Little Neck Bay to Fort Totten:** At its northern end, Alley is reduced to a thin green strip, a sort of forested buffer zone on either side of the Cross-Island Parkway. At the end of the North Run, at Cloverdale Boulevard, you can make a .8-mile circuit of Oakland Lake, a small, clean pond, and then continue north to the junction of Northern Boulevard and the Cross-Island Parkway. At the base of Little Neck Bay by the Alley Creek tidal flats, pick up the 3.4-mile bicycle-running path on the east side of the Cross-Island. This path continues past the Nichols Bayside Marina, past the pedestrian bridge over the Cross-Island to Crocheron Park, past Fort Totten, under the Throgs Neck Bridge, and on to Utopia Parkway. The course is flat, relatively free of potholes, and much used despite the noise and pollution generated by six lanes of speeding traffic. The running path amounts to the seventh lane of the Cross-Island, which shares its light to make night running possible and fairly safe. The views cross-bay to Douglaston, usually through and around the sails of small boats, are pleasant, though there is little shade. And to end up in any sort of Utopia is not half bad.

ALLEY PARK—MEASURED COURSES

2 miles	A + B	**plus**	.1 mile
3 miles	A + C + D	**plus**	.04 mile
3 miles	Barbieri loop (large)		
4 miles	(A + B) x 2	**plus**	.2 mile
4 miles	A + C + (D x 2)	minus	.08 mile
4 miles	B + C + D + E	minus	.18 mile
5 miles	(B x 2) + C + D	minus	.14 mile
5 miles	Barbieri loop (large) + A + B	**plus**	.1 mile
6 miles	(A + C + D) x 2	**plus**	.08 mile
8 miles	(A + C + D) x 2 + A + B	**plus**	.18 mile
10 miles	(A + B) x 2 + A + (C + D + E) x 2	**plus**	.02 mile

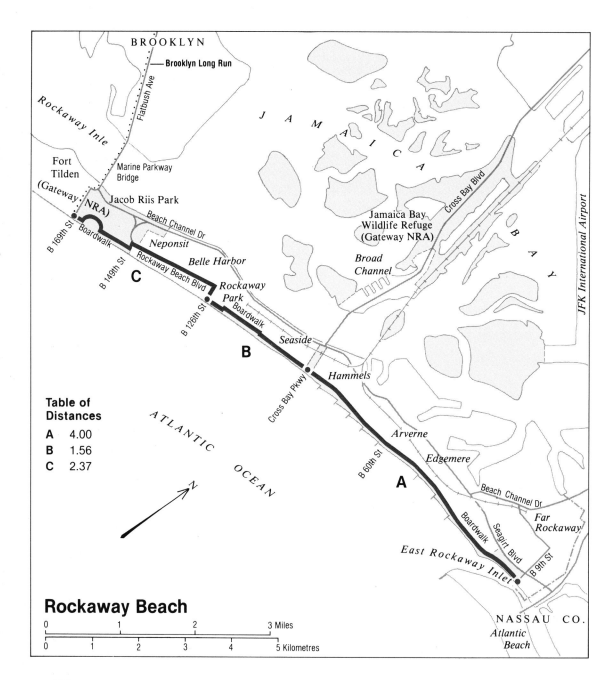

BROOKLYN

Brooklyn Long Run

Flatbush Ave

Rockaway Inle

J A M A I C A

Fort Tilden (Gateway NRA)

Marine Parkway Bridge

Jacob Riis Park

Beach Channel Dr

B 169th St

Boardwalk

Neponsit

B 149th St

Rockaway Beach Blvd

C

Belle Harbor

Rockaway Park

B 126th St

Boardwalk

Jamaica Bay Wildlife Refuge (Gateway NRA)

Broad Channel

Cross Bay Blvd

B A Y

JFK International Airport

B

Seaside

Cross Bay Pkwy

Hammels

Table of Distances
A   4.00
B   1.56
C   2.37

ATLANTIC

OCEAN

N

Arverne

Edgemere

B 60th St

A

Boardwalk

Seagirt Blvd

Beach Channel Dr

Far Rockaway

B 9th St

East Rockaway Inlet

Rockaway Beach

0   1   2   3 Miles

0   1   2   3   4   5 Kilometres

NASSAU CO.

Atlantic Beach

ROCKAWAY BEACH

5.5 miles

Once an exclusive resort, the Rockaways are now a summer resort of necessity for New York City's millions. There are apartments along the boardwalk that have the look of a failed attempt at a Rockaways Riviera, and behind the apartment buildings are weedy lots and the ramshackle elevated A train. The place has a forlorn, almost forsaken, quality, appropriate to a melancholy run, even on a sunny day. Plenty of runners use the 5.5-mile boardwalk for colorful sunrise and sunset workouts, though at any time of day the clean salt air and sea spray make for superior aerobic running. At some spots to the northwest, familiar skyscrapers are visible over the dune grass—Manhattan's, and miniatures at a 14-mile distance. The Rockaway Road Runners meet for a group run at Beach 106th on Saturdays at 8 A.M. and Sundays at 8:30 A.M. The Rockaways are a far-out, faraway place to run and, if run on other than summer weekends or holidays, give guarantee of a course far, far from the plodding crowd.

FOOTING: Mostly wooden boardwalk that is springy to the foot. Pay close attention to the boards, however, because much of this boardwalk is in need of restoration—only the most ravaged spots have been patched with new wood—and nailheads stick up here and there.

COURSE DIRECTIONS: Pick up the cement path to the boardwalk at Beach Ninth Street and head west. Continue on the boardwalk until it ends at Beach 126th Street (A + B).

HAZARDS: Strong winds that fling sand; chill from rising wind and sudden temperature drop (carry a windbreaker); sun zone, no shade; crowds of bathers on weekends and holidays (run early or late); safe for night running. If you run on the sand, watch for glass, shells, and tar.

COMFORTS: Exceptionally clean rest rooms along the boardwalk and at Jacob Riis Park; hot and cold showers for men and women at Jacob Riis; water fountains in both areas. Expect a breeze.

MASS TRANSPORT: I.N.D. Eighth Avenue A train to Beach Twenty-fifth Street and walk east to Beach Ninth Street; or A train to Beach 116th and walk west to Beach 126th Street; CC to Beach 116th Street.

EXTENSIONS: 1) Many runners add a 2.3-mile extension to the Rockaway Boardwalk Run by going right on Beach 126th, left on Rockaway Beach, left at Jacob Riis Park, and right onto the Riis Boardwalk (in fact, asphalt tile). The Jacob Riis Boardwalk ends at Beach 169th Street (C). 2) Beach 169th is the end of the 9.82-mile Coney Island–Sheepshead Bay–Shore Greenbelt Run—take Beach 169th north to Rockaway Point Road; cross Rockaway Point Road and continue on the sidewalk path across the Marine Parkway Bridge to Brooklyn. 3) Follow Cross Bay Boulevard from the Rockaway Boardwalk at Beach Ninety-fourth north across Jamaica Bay onto Woodhaven Boulevard, for an 8.5-mile connecting run to Forest Park.

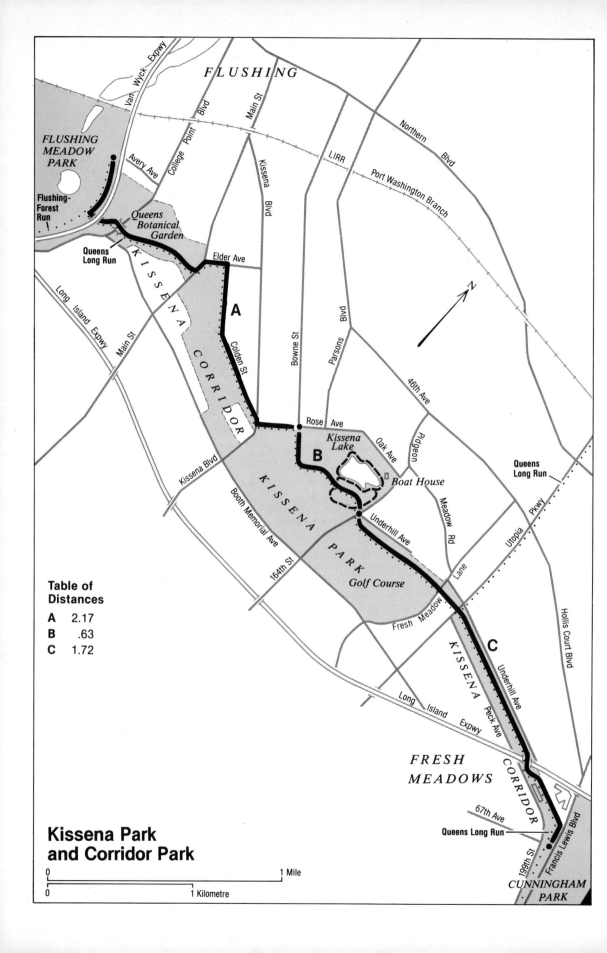

FLUSHING

FLUSHING MEADOW PARK

Flushing-Forest Run

Van Wyck Expwy

Avery Ave

College Point Blvd

Main St

Kissena Blvd

Northern Blvd

LIRR

Port Washington Branch

N

Queens Botanical Garden

Queens Long Run

KISSENA CORRIDOR

Elder Ave

A

Colden St

Bowne St

Parsons Blvd

46th Ave

Long Island Expwy

Main St

Kissena Blvd

Booth Memorial Ave

164th St

KISSENA PARK

Golf Course

Rose Ave

Kissena Lake

Oak Ave

Pidgeon

Boat House

B

Meadow Rd

Queens Long Run

Underhill Ave

Lane

Utopia Pkwy

Hollis Court Blvd

Fresh Meadow

KISSENA

C

Underhill Ave

Peck Ave

Long Island Expwy

CORRIDOR

FRESH MEADOWS

67th Ave

Queens Long Run

199th St

Francis Lewis Blvd

CUNNINGHAM PARK

Table of Distances

A   2.17
B   .63
C   1.72

Kissena Park and Corridor Park

0 ————————————— 1 Mile

0 ————————————— 1 Kilometre

KISSENA PARK AND CORRIDOR PARK

1.1 miles, Kissena Park
3.3 miles, Kissena Corridor Park

A neighborhood runner from Flushing or Fresh Meadows or Utopia might do a daily loop of Kissena Park, but an out-of-borough runner is only likely to come here en route to some larger park, say in doing the four miles between Flushing Meadow Park and Cunningham. Kissena Park is neat, tidy, and charming, as are the neighborhoods surrounding it. There is a 1.1-mile figure-eight course, though by trailing more complex patterns you can easily manage two miles with some variety—one modest hill, one modest swamp, one modest lake. Kissena Lake is spring-fed, and the park's trees of a stately age. The park is so small as to be free of roads, and therefore of cars. In dry weather, a .63-mile run is possible on a straight-line sandy trail that skirts a large swamp—of which it becomes a part during rains.

Kissena is the fat centerpiece of the Kissena Corridor Park, which begins at the Queens Botanical Garden, by Flushing Meadow Park, and continues on to Cunningham. A good green link.

FOOTING: Asphalt path in the park, smooth except on the south-central side where frequent marsh flooding has buried it under dirt and mud and caused it to crack up and disintegrate.

COURSE DIRECTIONS: Begin at the Avery Avenue entrance to Flushing Meadow Park (by the Taystee Bread time-and-temp. sign); proceed south and then east, to a pedestrian ramp that drops you in the back-forty apple orchard of the Queens Botanical Garden; pass through a gate just before the Bee Garden and on out to the main gate; cross Main Street and either pick a dog trail through the wild end of Kissena Corridor Park or follow Colden Road along the northern edge of the park to Rose Avenue; left on Rose; right into Kissena Park at Bowne (A); choice of looping left and around Kissena Lake for the figure-eight course or continuing more or less straight through on the sandy trail by the marsh (B); exit 164th and Underhill; follow Underhill along the north edge of Kissena Park Golf Course to Meadow Road, where the "developed" part of Kissena Corridor Park begins. Run on the sidewalk beside Underhill or Peck Avenue or on the paths through the corridor; at 196th Place cross over the Long Island Expressway on pedestrian walk; continue east to Francis Lewis Boulevard at about 67th Avenue (C); go south (right) on Francis Lewis, on the dirt path beside it, to 73rd Avenue; left on 73rd; right onto Hollis Court Boulevard to the start of the Old Motor Highway leading into Alley Park.

HAZARDS: Cars at the street crossings; cars pulling out from parking spots; night running not recommended for the lone woman runner.

COMFORTS: Rest rooms and water fountains in Kissena Park.

MASS TRANSPORT: I.R.T. No. 7 Flushing Line to Main Street. Walk or run .5 mile to the Avery Avenue entrance to Flushing Meadow Park. Street parking available.

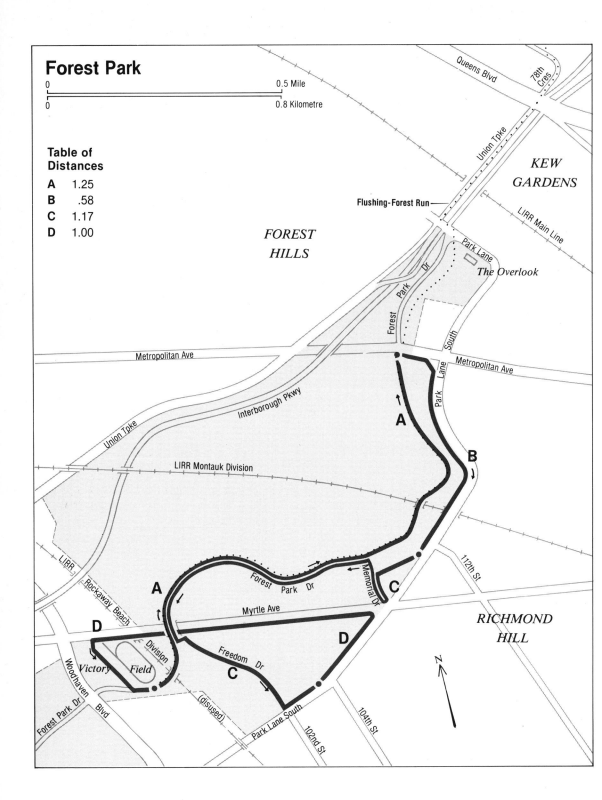

Forest Park

0 ———————————————————— 0.5 Mile

0 ———————————————————— 0.8 Kilometre

Table of Distances

A   1.25
B   .58
C   1.17
D   1.00

FOREST HILLS

KEW GARDENS

Queens Blvd

78th Cres

Union Tpke

LIRR Main Line

Flushing-Forest Run

Park Lane

The Overlook

Forest Park Dr

Park Lane South

Metropolitan Ave

Metropolitan Ave

Interborough Pkwy

Union Tpke

LIRR Montauk Division

Park Lane

A

B

112th St

LIRR

Rockaway Beach

Forest Park Dr

Memorial Dr

C

RICHMOND HILL

A

Myrtle Ave

D

Division

D

Freedom Dr

C

Victory Field

Woodhaven Blvd

Forest Park Dr

(disused)

Park Lane South

102nd St

104th St

N

FOREST PARK

4 miles

Forest Park is the running preserve of the Forest Hills and Kew Gardens gentry, and of Queens' own ultramarathon élite. A first visit to Forest is rather awesome—that such a small park is the site of one of New York's most famous ultramarathons of 40 miles. (In 1979, a 100 km, twenty-loop race was staged here as well.) The course is just four miles long—and that only by a prodigious sleight-of-route that traces the shape of a butterfly but leaves the forest for the streets too often to be called pure woods running. Try Forest a second time. White arrows painted on the ground take some of the trickiness out of the route, but there is much backing and forthing, looping and hairpin turning, and when you consider doing it ten times over, let alone *twenty*, the thought of all that tedium becomes almost pernicious. The course snakes through the woods on Forest Park Drive, then follows a sidewalk, then a dirt path, then an asphalt path, for a challenging variety of footings. While doing your laps you might meditate on what the meaning of the mini-ultra-marathon is or where the 40-miler's wall is. The street scenes surrounding Forest Park are mostly Queens Tudor England.

FOOTING: A variety of surfaces (asphalt, dirt, concrete, tree roots to navigate, curbs to hop); generally flat with a few small bumps. Forest sits on the crest of the terminal moraine that runs up Long Island.

COURSE DIRECTIONS: Tricky: Start at the mark on Forest Park Drive opposite the 440-yard track (the start for the 4-mile, 40-mile, and 100 km races); follow Forest Park Drive to Metropolitan Avenue (A); go right on sidewalk beside park till you are opposite house No. 109-50 on Park Lane South (B); there turn right into park on asphalt path; follow a white arrow; at pond, notice 2-mile mark painted on path; turn left off sidewalk at big ten-foot-tall cedar post. Go left at 102nd (C) and Park Lane on sidewalk (just before 104th, notice 3-mile mark painted on path); go left off Woodhaven sidewalk at the 440-yard track; and left onto Forest Park Drive, return to start (D).

OTHER RUNS: 1) There is a 440-yard cinder track at Victory Field. 2) Part of the course can be done on the bridle path beside Forest Park Drive.

HAZARDS: Women are well advised not to run the course unless accompanied by a man (at 10 A.M. one summer morning in 1978, a woman runner was attacked by two men wielding hatchets); automobiles; losing the trail (pay close attention, and be patient while awaiting the next white arrow).

COMFORTS: Rest rooms and fountains at Forest Park headquarters. Showers and lockers for men (the women's facilities are full of painting equipment).

MASS TRANSPORT: I.N.D. E and F trains to Union Turnpike; B.M.T. J train to Elderts Lane, Forest Parkway, Woodhaven Boulevard, 102nd Street or 111th Street; street parking available.

EXTENSION: There is a 2.5-mile run south and west skirting the Forest Park Golf Course and then through and around the Cemetery Mile to the Ridgewood Reservoir.

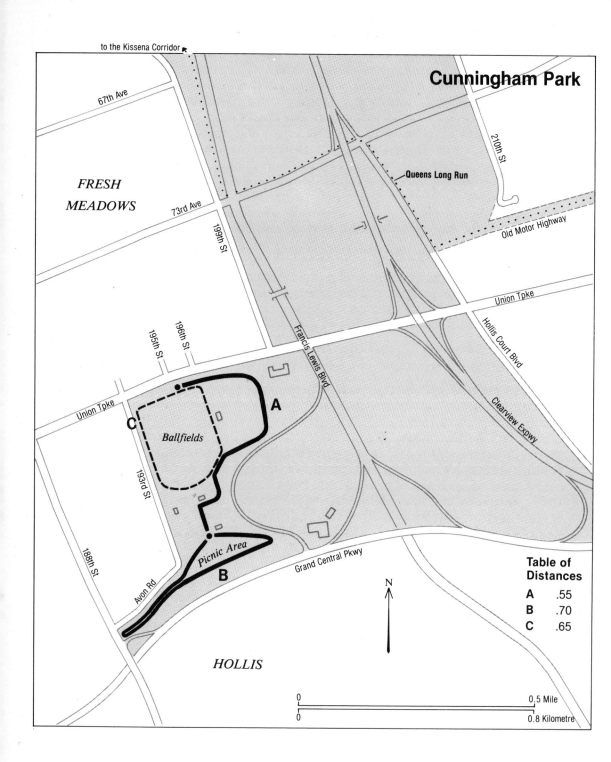

to the Kissena Corridor

Cunningham Park

67th Ave

210th St

FRESH
MEADOWS

73rd Ave

Queens Long Run

199th St

Old Motor Highway

Union Tpke

196th St

195th St

Francis Lewis Blvd

Hollis Court Blvd

Union Tpke

Clearview Expwy

C

A

Ballfields

193rd St

Picnic Area

188th St

B

Avon Rd

Grand Central Pkwy

N

HOLLIS

Table of
Distances

A   .55
B   .70
C   .65

0   0.5 Mile
0   0.8 Kilometre

CUNNINGHAM PARK

.65 and 1.8 miles

Cunningham Park is a large forested park named for W. Arthur Cunningham, the City Comptroller for four decades from 1894 to 1934, but it was parkwayed and expresswayed to bits by Robert Moses in his forty-*four*-year heyday. No fewer than six major thoroughfares cut through Cunningham, not to mention several two-lane roads. As a result, the southwestern quadrant is the only part of the park in which much running is done. There, runners have a choice of a .65-mile asphalt loop around ball fields or an out-and-back asphalt trail of .55 mile that connects to a .7-mile dirt cross-country trail through an oak woods. This part of the course is used regularly in season by local high-school cross-country teams.

The rest of Cunningham is shot through with trails, mostly used by teen-age trailbikers, but available to runners who feel like exploring the woods. If Cunningham is not a great running area, it has a lot of backwoods potential, especially for adventuresome freestyle runners who are not hung up on exact measurements and like the idea of exploring trails that will end up somewhere in the Queens unknown.

FOOTING: Asphalt path; cross-country course, a combination of cinder, gravel, dirt, and leaf mulch, also tree roots, small gullies, and rocks—much unevenness.

COURSE DIRECTIONS: Begin where the asphalt paths form a T near 195th Street and Union Turnpike. Head west on the asphalt path across the parking lot by the tennis courts; note arrows on pavement; follow the ball-field loop for about forty yards; then follow the yellow, red, and blue arrows around the upper parking lot; at the southwest corner of the lot, head into the woods through a jumble of picnic tables (this trail is well blazed in red and yellow paint), continue to 188th Street and Avon Road; on the return, just after a large tree in the middle of the trail, bear right for the upper part of the cross-country trail; take a sharp left back to the loop's point of origin—path still clearly blazed. Look for the word KICK painted on a stone at the turn; from the parking lot retrace the course to the start.

HAZARDS: Unleashed dogs; trailbikes; poison ivy; short, steep, sometimes slippery pitches on the cross-country course; horses (there is a mounted police unit nearby); deserted woods that should be avoided by lone women runners; ball-field loop O.K. for night running.

COMFORTS: Rest rooms, showers, and fountains at park headquarters near the tennis courts.

MASS TRANSPORT: I.N.D. E or F train to Kew Gardens/Union Turnpike station, Q44A bus to park; plenty of parking.

EXTENSIONS: 1) Follow Union Turnpike east; right on Hollis Court Boulevard to pick up the 1.9-mile Old Motor Highway to Alley Park. 2) 1.72 miles north from Francis Lewis Boulevard and west through Kissena Corridor Park: Kissena Park.

QUEENS MINI-RUNS

SPRINGFIELD PARK: There is a .25-mile loop through this tiny park in southeast Queens, created around a spring-fed lake. Piles of garbage provide the background motif, with lots of "No Dumping" signs. Jets roar overhead. The lake is used by model-boat enthusiasts and is crowded on weekends. Except for nearby residents, not many people use the park for running. Running in pairs is recommended. Rest rooms on the premises.

BROOKVILLE PARK: A tabloid Clove Lakes-style park with two instead of three lakes. A 1.3-mile loop is possible by running a figure-eight course around the two lakes. Safe for lone women runners. Crowded with picnickers and day campers during the summer. Usually there's a good breeze off the ponds, and jet noise overhead. Rest rooms for men and women.

BAISLEY POND PARK: Largest of the southeast Queens parks, Baisley Pond is the community fishing hole, a spring-fed lake in which carp, catfish, and sunnies can be found. Sticking to the glass-littered asphalt path by the pond, a runner can do 1.2 miles, with an additional .35-mile loop around the ball fields at the northern end of the park. Baisley Pond is sometimes used for between-flight runs by airline crews flying out of Kennedy, which is about ten blocks distant. Travelers stopping over at J.F.K. might want to do this course for lack of anything handier. Pleasant breeze off the pond, lots of birdsong. Not safe for the lone woman runner. Clean rest rooms open year round.

CROCHERON PARK: A 1.3-mile bluff-toploop overlooking Little Neck Bay. The run is over smooth asphalt, and the large loop of the park can be made to include a few hills. In hilly places where there is a choice between steps or grass, choose grass. After circling this tidy park, you can cross over the Cross-Island Parkway on a pedestrian bridge and drop down a flight of stairs to pick up the Little Neck–Fort Totten portion of the Queens Long Run.

COLLEGE POINT: The running hotbed of the College Point peninsula is a park suffering an identity crisis. Located at the tip of the peninsula, the park is known as Chisolm Park by old-timers, MacNeil or McNeil by almost everyone else in College Point, and as College Point Shore Front Park on most maps. Whatever its name, it is a delightful park for runners, offering well-paved asphalt trails, marked half-mile and full-mile courses, shore views and breezes, fountains that work, and rest rooms. The marked routes are used for age-group races sponsored by the local College Point Athletic Club. The park is considered safe for lone women runners in daylight. The routes start at 119th Street and Fifth Avenue and take in a few short but challenging hills. The College Point Athletic Club, which recently sponsored a half-marathon that attracted more than twelve hundred runners, supports a great deal of running throughout Queens. The club holds a weekly run every Saturday at 10:00 A.M. which begins at the park entrance. College Pointers uphold the notion that Queens is a series of smaller communities. They are College Pointers, *sui generis*, and pride themselves on the small-town atmosphere. According to one of the locals, if there were a real Archie Bunker, he'd live in College Point. Take the I.R.T. No. 7 Flushing Line to Main Street, Q25 or Q34 bus to College Point.

TRIBOROUGH BRIDGE: The Triborough Bridge run is one of *the* runners' highs in New York City. New York's master builder, Robert Moses, considered that of all his bridges, the view of Manhattan from the Triborough was the best. The pedestrian run-way, about twenty feet higher than the roadway, puts the runner some 163 feet above the East River. The two-mile concrete walk is narrow and in some places crumbling. There is nothing higher than a three-and-a-half-foot railing between the runner and the churning waters of the Hell Gate. A runner doing the Triborough in the midst of a summer lightning storm reported seeing death and deciding that—if this was it—O.K. The Triborough adventure is for the stouthearted only. It should not be run in any kind of wind or in winter ice conditions. It's one slip on the ice and into the Hell Gate. Before ascending the north or south walk from Astoria or Randall's Island, check the prevailing breeze and run so that exhaust pollution is carried away from you.

ASTORIA PARK: Tucked between the pillars of the Triborough and the Hell Gate railroad bridge in far west Queens is a neighborhood runner's haven, Astoria Park. Here is a well-used .25-mile cinder track, a 1.25-mile asphalt loop just inside the park perimeter, a nice breeze, and views of the waters of the Hell Gate. The 1.25-mile loop can be started and finished at any point. For resistance work there is a short, steep hill at the first land-based arch of the railroad bridge. The park is generally thought safe for all runners, and some sections, especially the track, get enough light for safe night running. Astoria is recommended for automobile-dependent runners who need to put in a workout during the day. There is easy access from the Hoyt Avenue exit of the Grand Central Parkway. There is solar-warmed water for showering (men and women) at the Morty Arkin Memorial Field House. Also water fountains and lockers (bring own lock). To reach Astoria Park take the B.M.T. RR train to Astoria Boulevard–Hoyt Avenue and Thirty-first Street and walk five blocks west on Hoyt Avenue South. Street parking available. At Hoyt Avenue and Twenty-seventh Street, pick up the pedestrian walkway over the Triborough Bridge for the 1.89-mile run to Randall's Island.

RIDGEWOOD RESERVOIR: In Highland Park, on the roof of Queens, is a 1.2-mile loop that follows the contours of the Ridgewood Reservoir. The asphalt trail is so deeply scored in sections as to discourage most bicyclists. The ruts are of little consequence for runners, and there is not much glass. The view is Depression-red-brick tenement over the low-rise rooftops and TV antennas of south Queens and east New York, in Brooklyn. A breeze generally blows off the water except where the reservoir loop comes close to the Interborough Parkway to the north. A caved-in cave-in, once fenced off, has created a local swimming hole, though the police try diligently to chase young Huck Finns away. The reservoir is a favored Sunday morning jaunt for the Flushing Meadow Track Club, 15 miles round trip. The reservoir loop is not recommended for lone women runners or for night running. The water fountains along Vermont Place down the eastern bank from the reservoir work. No rest rooms functioning, however. B.M.T. J train to Cleveland Street (at Fulton) and walk three blocks north.

FLUSHING MEADOW—FOREST PARK: For the 5-mile run to the start of the Forest Park course, head south from the Taystee Bread parking lot, keeping Meadow Lake to the right. Cross Jewel Avenue (1.94 miles). Go right a short distance and then left on a dirt trail south that leaves Willow Lake to your left. Near the end of Willow, after some swamp running, go right and pick up the steps for the pedestrian overpass of the Grand Central Parkway (near the I.N.D. subway yard). Go up a switchback and cross Queens Boulevard (1.01 miles). Continue straight, running against traffic, on Union Turnpike to Park Lane. Go left on Park Lane for twenty yards, then right onto Forest Park Drive. Cross Metropolitan Avenue (.59 mile) and continue on Forest Park Drive (1.34 miles) to the start of the 4-mile Forest Park Run, near Woodhaven Boulevard. Another .2 mile, at the comfort-station water fountain across Woodhaven Boulevard, gives a precise 5-mile extension. (The alternate winter and rain route from Flushing Meadow begins at the same place. But go *left* on Jewel Avenue. Head east, go right onto Main Street; after about a mile on Main Street go right onto the service road of the Grand Central Parkway; cross Queens Boulevard and continue on Union Turnpike, as on the other course.) And a 2.5-mile extender of this run is a straight cemetery run southwest to the Ridgewood Reservoir at Highland Park on the Brooklyn border.

THE BRONX

The Bronx is mainland America, and the rest of New York City is not. In 1931, Ogden Nash dismissed the Bronx with "No thonx!" Several decades later, he softened to "The Bronx? God bless them!" There are, in fact, so many Bronx that it's probably incorrect to refer to them as one. Their running takes place in the northern tier of themselves and not at all in the south, except on New York City Marathon day, when Mile 20 passes through the South Bronx and marathoners are encouraged over the wall by authentic Bronx cheers.

Nowadays, New York running means Manhattan, Central Park, but as recently as twenty-five years ago it meant the Bronx, and specifically the Macomb's Dam Park area—the 440-yard cinder track by Yankee Stadium, the sidewalk around the stadium and on Sedgwick Avenue. The annual Cherry Tree Marathon, now defunct, was held here as a tune-up for the Boston Marathon. Staged close to February 22 and honoring George Washington's alleged inability to tell a lie, the five-loop race started at Yankee Stadium and included steep hills and sharp right-angle turns. Other races were run around Yankee Stadium and through the nearby Bronx Terminal Market. In the late 1950's, the area began to run down, and as the ability to dodge rocks and bottles became a necessary running skill, Macomb's runners left for safer courses. Miles Jackson, of the Macomb's Dam Sports Association, wants to rebuild the area and provide a lighted track. It's ironic that the city has spent more than a hundred million dollars to rebuild Yankee Stadium for professional (spectator) sports when it would take relatively little to begin to restore Macomb's Dam Park as a running center.

Van Cortlandt Park in the Bronx is the traditional home of cross-country running in the United States. The famed five-mile course has had the ungrudging respect of runners for more than eighty years, and the route's notorious high spot, Vault Hill — a narrow sidewinder — shows no signs of wearing down to a gentle old age, despite heavy foot erosion. In Van Cortlandt, the runner can explore the city's only aqueduct run—a three-mile wooded segment on the Old Croton Aqueduct path.

Nowadays, with running coming back to the Bronx and runners coming to the Bronx, these parks make an ideal destination for a long run from Manhattan and an interesting change of place. For the Bronx are well connected— by bridges, to Manhattan; by trails, to Westchester; and by parkway greenbelts east-west, north-south, intra borough.

For instance, if Riverdale is too much the suburbs countrified, and its small but persistent hills are not enough of a challenge, the runner can strike out due east and eight miles later be in Pelham Bay Park, the city's largest, greenest, most oceanic park, possessed of several notable urban wonders. The most obvious, because until recently it could be smelled before it could be seen, is Garbage Mountain. An unrunnable but unique topographic feature, it has been a growing mound on the landscape nurtured by the Department of Sanitation. Garbage Mountain was closed to garbage early in 1979 before it had topped out Todt Hill on Staten Island as the city's highest point and has been seeded to grass and may be developed as a hill course. The other urban wonder, on Hunter's Island, is the city's only trailside mineral spring, New York's Lourdes, if you will, for runners and health nuts who prefer the taste to Perrier, and portage it home in large plastic bottles. The Pacers of Pelham Bay Park under the direction of Cahit Yeter have designed and carefully marked (in yellow paint) the city's longest, most Thoreauvian runners' nature trail — a 10-mile refresher course in flowers and fields, birds and berries, tidepools and beaches — the things you're supposed to have to get away from the city to find. If Pelham Bay Park is the Bronx, the Bronx is the *Symphonie Pastorale*.

And that is not all. The Bronx has a Historical Society that puts on an annual 5-mile historical run. And Joe Kleinerman, the elder statesman of New York City running and the Chaucerian raconteur of New York running lore, lives in the Bronx. His team, the Millrose Athletic Association, one of the oldest competitive clubs in the United States and the only American team ever to win the 52.5-mile London-to-Brighton race, holds its monthly meeting at the pleasantly Bronxian Terminal Bar, on Broadway across from Van Cortlandt Park, where many of its members train. Dr. Norb Sander, the world-class Masters runner, is a member of Millrose and a Bronx runner whose Preventive and Sports Medicine Center is located just off the Pelham Bay Park trail, on City Island. The center's staff, made up of specialists in a number of areas, is geared particularly to runners and their myriad stress syndromes — a place, if you can't find it in Manhattan, where doctors understand the injuries of excellence, because they themselves are athletes.

And for the botanical runner the Bronx provides the landscapes of the New York Botanical Garden — modeled on the Royal Botanical Gardens at Kew, England — a run through what seems like a private garden, a run that is like a 3.5-mile vacation from the city.

The Bronx always has been the borough for runners, and more and more lower New Yorkers are beginning to realize its richness. They are heading up to the top of the city, crossing one of the many bridges to the Bronx mainland. The born-again runners of the 1980's have begun to discover the Bronx, God bless them. And they have tied it all together with the 24.5-mile Bronx Long Run, a sort of underdone marathon.

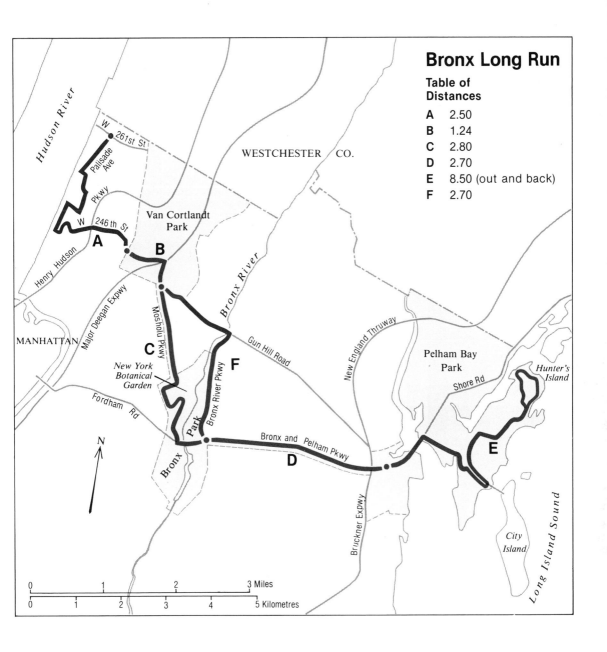

Bronx Long Run

Table of Distances

A	2.50
B	1.24
C	2.80
D	2.70
E	8.50 (out and back)
F	2.70

Hudson River

W 261st St

WESTCHESTER CO.

Palisade Ave

Van Cortlandt Park

Pkwy

W 246th St

Bronx River

A

B

Henry Hudson

Major Deegan Expwy

Mosholu Pkwy

New England Thruway

MANHATTAN

C

Gun Hill Road

Pelham Bay Park

Shore Rd

Hunter's Island

New York Botanical Garden

F

Fordham Rd

Bronx River Pkwy

Bronx and Pelham Pkwy

E

Bronx Park

D

Long Island Sound

N

Bruckner Expwy

City Island

0	1	2	3 Miles
0	1 2 3 4		5 Kilometres

VAN CORTLANDT PARK

5 miles

Van Cortlandt Park is the choice running place for the majority of Bronx runners, as well as one of the historic places of pilgrimage for the religious runner. Its famous 5-mile varsity cross-country course was the first such in this country. Van Cortlandt (if you can spell it right, you can probably run it) has been the site of annual elementary-school, high-school, and college competitions, including the IC4As, for decades. In addition, the Metropolitan A.A.U. and the New York Road Runners Club hold races here. Nearly every famous runner in the United States has run this rugged course at one time or another.

The Van Cortlandt courses appear to have been designed by a mathematician who favored the loop as the basic unit of run. You can stick to the big zero, the Parade Ground, for 1.4 flat miles. For distance, you do running-by-addition and keep adding loops. Add Vault Hill for 1.7 miles and a rugged climb; add Vault Hill plus the backhills loop for 3.3 miles. Add another loop of the Parade Ground and Freshman Hill for the classic 5. The backwoods loop has a rigorous topography of gullies and ravines along an eroded dirt path. Some of the last of the Mohicans hunted here and you can still flush pheasants, rabbits, and chipmunks, and sometimes the early morning runner catches the quick red fox. Vault Hill, which holds the Van Cortlandt family remains (Jacobus Van Cortlandt was Mayor of New York, 1710–19), is where the city records were hidden from the British during the Revolution. There is a 100-foot climb from chute to summit and endless opportunities to misplant a foot, twist an ankle, or skin a knee. Some resistance buffs run repeats of Vault Hill the way other runners do intervals, as if to reenact the myth of Sisyphus. This is a course that makes strong runners walk, upon occasion. The Van Cortlandt Track Club holds a group run every Saturday, assembling at 242nd Street and Broadway at 9 A.M. in summer, 9:30 A.M. in fall and winter for runs of from 5 to 15 miles.

FOOTING: Cinder track supplemented with ground glass and dirt around the Parade Ground; soft dirt track; erosion, exposed roots, rocks, and soft sand on the back loop; keep your eyes and your feet on the ground.

COURSE DIRECTIONS: The classic 5-mile course starts at the southwest corner of the Parade Ground. Go east on the cowpath, a trail worn through the grass that passes the Van Cortlandt Manor. Go left at a turn-pole (A), then right at the chute (D) and up and around Freshman Hill to the bridge over the Henry Hudson Parkway (E). Continue north, over the bridge, on a washboard course. The narrow trail makes passing difficult here (H). At the end of the loop cross over the bridge again, heading south. Downhill (F) to the flats for another spin around the Parade Ground (C + A) and back into the chute (D). This time go left off the Freshman Hill trail for the Vault Hill switchback (G), which comes around the 4-mile mark. Once over the summit drop down to the flats again for the .5-mile on the Parade Ground track to the finish (F + C).

OTHER RUNS: .25-mile cinder track at Van Cortlandt Stadium.

HAZARDS: The remoteness of some of the back trails can make them unsafe: in 1978, a rapist dressed as a runner attacked four lone women in the park's northern section, then was finally caught during a fifth rape attempt because his victim was the N.Y.P.D.'s Muggable Mary. No night running except on the flats parallel to Broadway and on the lighted asphalt paths near the stadium; many dogs off leash turn the course near Broadway into their personal latrine; the Parade Ground swarms with baseball, softball, soccer, rugby, hurling, and cricket players, as well as picnickers and errant children on summer weekends.

COMFORTS: Fountains and hot showers for men and women year round at Van Cortlandt Stadium; two water fountains at the beginning of the back loop on the cross-country course.

MASS TRANSPORT: Seventh Avenue I.R.T. local No. 1 to 242nd Street and Broadway. Any northbound Broadway bus. Parking available on the street, at the golf-course parking lot off Van Cortlandt Park South, or at the Mosholu Avenue entrance, near the stables.

EXTENSIONS: 1) A 1-mile run west on West 246th, from Broadway, connects with the Riverdale–Palisade Avenue Run. 2) A 2.5-mile run east from 242nd and Broadway and south on the Mosholu Parkway leads to the New York Botanical Garden Run.

VAN CORTLANDT PARK—MEASURED COURSES

2 miles	A + D + G + F + C	**plus** .03 mile
3 miles	A + D + E + H + F + C	**plus** .02 mile
4 miles	A + D + E + H + F + C + A + B + F + E	minus .16 mile
4 miles	A + D + E + H + F + C + A + D + E	**plus** .02 mile
4 miles	(A + D + G + F + C) x 2	**plus** .06 mile
5 miles	A + D + G + F + C + A + D + E + H + F + C	**plus** .05 mile
6 miles	A + D + G + F + C + A + D + E + H + F + C + A + D + E + F	minus .09 mile
8 miles	(A + D + G + F + C) x 4	**plus** .12 mile
10 miles	(A + D + G + F + C) x 5	**plus** .15 mile
12 miles	(A + D + G + F + C) x 6	**plus** .18 mile

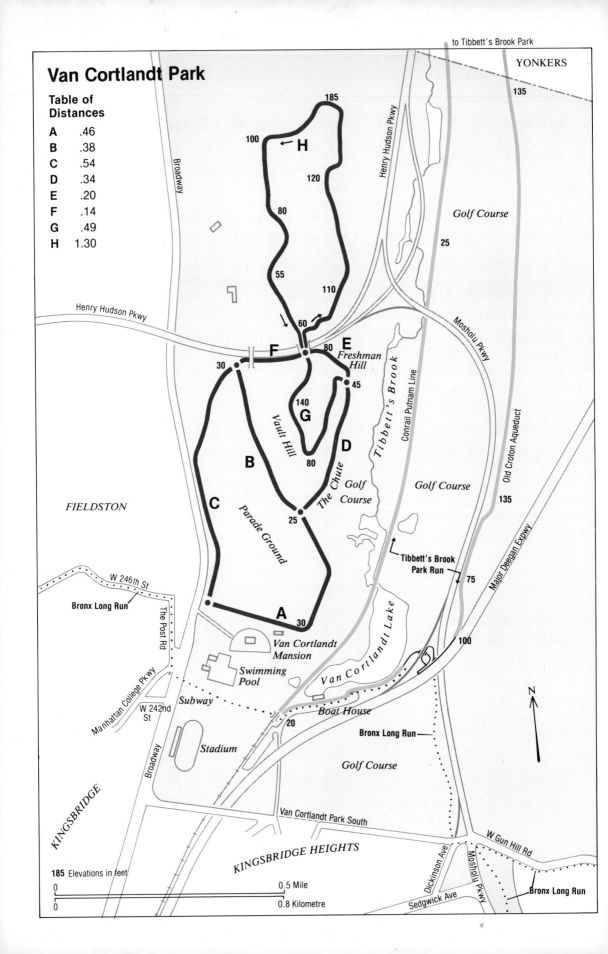

Van Cortlandt Park

Table of Distances

A	.46
B	.38
C	.54
D	.34
E	.20
F	.14
G	.49
H	1.30

YONKERS

to Tibbett's Brook Park

135

185

100

H

120

80

55

110

60

Golf Course

25

Henry Hudson Pkwy

Mosholu Pkwy

Broadway

Henry Hudson Pkwy

F

80

E

Freshman Hill

30

45

140

G

80

Vault Hill

B

The Chute

D

Tibbett's Brook

Conrail Putnam Line

Golf Course

Old Croton Aqueduct

FIELDSTON

Golf Course

135

C

Parade Ground

25

A

30

Tibbett's Brook Park Run

75

Major Deegan Expwy

Bronx Long Run

W 246th St

The Post Rd

Van Cortlandt Mansion

Swimming Pool

Van Cortlandt Lake

100

Manhattan College Pkwy

Subway

W 242nd St

Boat House

Bronx Long Run

20

N

Broadway

Stadium

Golf Course

KINGSBRIDGE

Van Cortlandt Park South

W Gun Hill Rd

KINGSBRIDGE HEIGHTS

Dickinson Ave

Mosholu Pkwy

185 Elevations in feet

0   0.5 Mile

0   0.8 Kilometre

Sedgwick Ave

Bronx Long Run

VAN CORTLANDT PARK—CROTON AQUEDUCT

7 miles

This is a quiet, shady run north out of Van Cortlandt Park along Conrail's Putnam Line tracks. The runner passes occasional bird-watchers and birds, for this is one of the city's known birding areas. At Tibbett's Brook Park, in Yonkers, there is a measured and marked 1.5-mile loop around the lake and meadow. The return to Van Cortlandt is on the last miles of the Old Croton Aqueduct, through a great wood. The Aqueduct (1837–42) was New York City's first outside source of drinking water. Note the old red brick access towers along the way. Occasionally you catch the sound of running water.

FOOTING: Cinder and bark beside railroad tracks and flat, though tie-hopping is necessary in a few spots because of narrow, rocky grade crossing and outreaching poison ivy; asphalt path in Tibbett's Brook Park; firm dirt path on the Aqueduct, wide enough for two abreast in most places; sometimes rocky; muddy in low ground after rains; mostly flat with a few small hills.

COURSE DIRECTIONS: Go east across the Parade Ground, or follow yellow arrows east on the asphalt path from 242nd and Broadway, to an abandoned railroad station just south of Van Cortlandt Lake. The run begins here. Go north beside the tracks for three miles, passing stone monoliths that were building-stone samples for Grand Central Terminal. Pass Van Cortlandt Lake and swamp. A hundred yards before a pedestrian overpass turn right and enter Tibbett's Brook Park through a hole in the chain link fence. Go right around the lake and north around the meadow. Turn east (left) in front of the park-headquarters building and cross Teresa Street. Climb a hill to the left. Go right onto the Croton Aqueduct path. Follow the aqueduct trail south, cross McLean Avenue, and reenter Van Cortlandt Park. The trail ends with a right turn onto an asphalt path that descends a hill close to the Mosholu Parkway, then climbs a hill to a bridge on the Major Deegan Expressway that crosses the Mosholu. Descend the stairs at the end of the bridge, turn left, and continue to the lake. Parallel the lake and return to the abandoned railroad station.

HAZARDS: The twice-a-week freight train that uses the tracks (the two weekdays on which the train makes its out-and-back run are not set—the only certainty is that a train seen heading out will return within twelve hours); horses beside the tracks; mosquitoes; poison ivy.

COMFORTS: Rest rooms and fountains in Van Cortlandt and Tibbett's Brook Parks.

MASS TRANSPORT: Same as for Van Cortlandt Park.

PELHAM BAY PARK

5 and 10 miles, Cahit Yeter Trail
4 miles, Golf Course Trail

Cahit Yeter, ultramarathoner and guiding spark of the Cahit Pacers, whose home turf is Pelham Bay Park, has laid out an idyllic nature run here. Cahit was born in Turkey, and his running tends toward the poetic: "You can run without fear here, without anything in mind but Nature. It is the most romantical place to run. At sunset, with the light filtering through the trees, the runner's high is here." The Cahit Yeter Trail, which is seventy percent on cinder and seventy-five percent in shade, begins quite ordinarily at the parking lot at Rice Stadium, passes through a meadow, bypasses Garbage Mountain (the volcano-shaped creation of the Department of Sanitation), and continues through and around the rocky New England-like shoreline of Hunter's Island. The runner is likely to flush pheasants, fishermen, an occasional hermit—several are reported to live in the park—or an amorous couple. Shore birds wade in the tide pools. The runner's foot plants run to violets and wild geranium in spring, day lilies in summer. The Cahit Pacers have found and excavated a mineral spring on Hunter's Island to which health pilgrims bring plastic bottles to fill and carry home.

Pelham, at two thousand acres, is the city's largest ocean–forest park, with wide-open views of Long Island Sound, City Island, boats, and islets. There is also a rugged cross-country bridle path course, around the park golf courses, whereon the runner is challenged by bogs, marshes, rivulets, quickmud, rutted paths, and general slop after a rain. Of the city's major parks, it is possibly the most foreign to citizens of the other boroughs. Yet for the runner, Pelham is a large breath of fresh air, having cornered much of the city's most wholesome and most aromatic. About a thousand people run Pelham every day. The Cahit Pacers meet every evening at five-thirty at Rice Stadium. Tuesdays and Thursdays, they do speedwork on the .25-mile track, and roadwork up to 20 miles on the other nights. On Saturdays, they meet at 9 A.M. for a 10-mile fun run and breakfast. Look for their T-shirts.

FOOTING: Seventy percent cinder, thirty percent asphalt and concrete, some rocky bridle path; at Orchard Beach, path becomes firmly packed dirt-cinder with only occasional rocks and tree roots to look out for; a few fallen tree trunks to hop over; a few streams to ford by plank; fairly rugged in spots.

COURSE DIRECTIONS: Cahit Yeter Trail: Begin at the parking lot at Rice Stadium (A), Ohm and Watt Streets, and follow the Cahit Pacers' yellow arrows, painted on the asphalt, or the yellow dots painted on the tree trunks. The path is explicit since both miles and quarter-miles are marked, and the mile markers are a foot square. At two places, 2 miles (B) and 9.75 miles (G), the Pacers have marked fartlek segments of 220 yards, in white paint, and signs are posted: "Speed Zone Ahead." Elsewhere, the Pacers have left messages—at 1.5 miles (B), "Have a nice run"; at 2.5 miles (D), "Say hi to a runner"; at 5.2 miles (F), "Don't stress"; and at 6 miles (E), "Run easy."

Golf Course Trail: Run starts on the Shore Road bridle path across the road from the golfers' parking field, a mile from Orchard Beach (J + D). The first mile is through the marshland around the Bartow-Pell Mansion and the Lagoon, with reedy views of the shore, shore birds, and Hunter's Island, as well as of rusting car carcasses. Near the 1-mile point, the bridle path meets Shore Road again. Turn right and stay beside Shore Road for .33 mile. At a parking lot just before a hill, turn left where a fire hydrant is buried in weeds on left side of road. The remaining three miles is along the fence line of the Split Rock and Pelham Golf Courses. Pick up the bridle trail, which continues right in obvious fashion through deep woods, skirts a few sylvan back yards, carries you over railroad tracks (H), parallels the New England Thruway and Hutchinson River Parkway for a bit, curves left, and passes under the railroad tracks, to the golfers' parking field (I). This run is not recommended for beginners, the faint of foot, or the urban runner who feels unsure on anything less regular than a perfectly smooth asphalt roadway. It is a trail far better suited to horses than to runners. There are many ways to be tripped up here—tree roots, pits in the path, mud holes, and small ponds that must be forded when the course floods after a rain; thick muck; some rocky sections. There is poison ivy in abundance in summer; mosquitoes; trail bikes; horses. No night running.

OTHER RUNS: 1) Orchard Beach Boardwalk (K), a crescent outlining the back beach, measures a fraction over 1 mile, end to end. The boardwalk is in fact asphalt tile, which provides a hard, somwhat uneven footing. The distance can be run on the sand at low tide, but wear shoes as there are glass and shells in abundance. 2) .5-mile oval drive at the Orchard Beach headquarters. 3) .5-mile path around Twin Islands (L), an offshoot from the Cahit Yeter Trail on Hunter's Island. 4) .25-mile track at Rice Stadium. 5) Cahit Yeter plans to develop a hill course on Garbage Mountain which was closed to trash in February 1979, and then seeded with grass. The smell is gone, and the distance around the base is 1.5 miles.

HAZARDS: Poison ivy in summer; mosquitoes; occasional cars or motor-bikes on the back trail; twenty-four-hour police protection, but park is not recommended for the lone woman runner, or for anyone after dark; Orchard Beach area overpopulated on weekends and holidays, but the rest of the park never seems to be.

Pelham Bay Park

Table of Distances

A	1.00
B	1.34
C	.72
D	.41
E	.67
F	1.37
G	1.35
H	2.15
I	1.81
J	1.00
K	1.00
L	.50

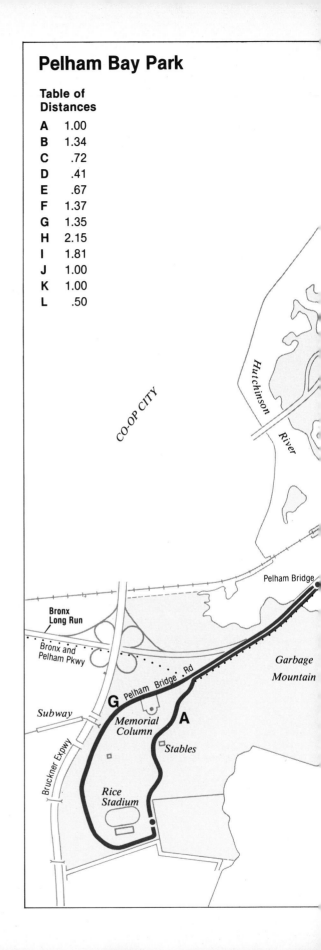

CO-OP CITY

Hutchinson River

Pelham Bridge

Bronx Long Run

Bronx and Pelham Pkwy

Pelham Bridge Rd

Garbage Mountain

G

Subway

Memorial Column

A

Stables

Bruckner Expwy

Rice Stadium

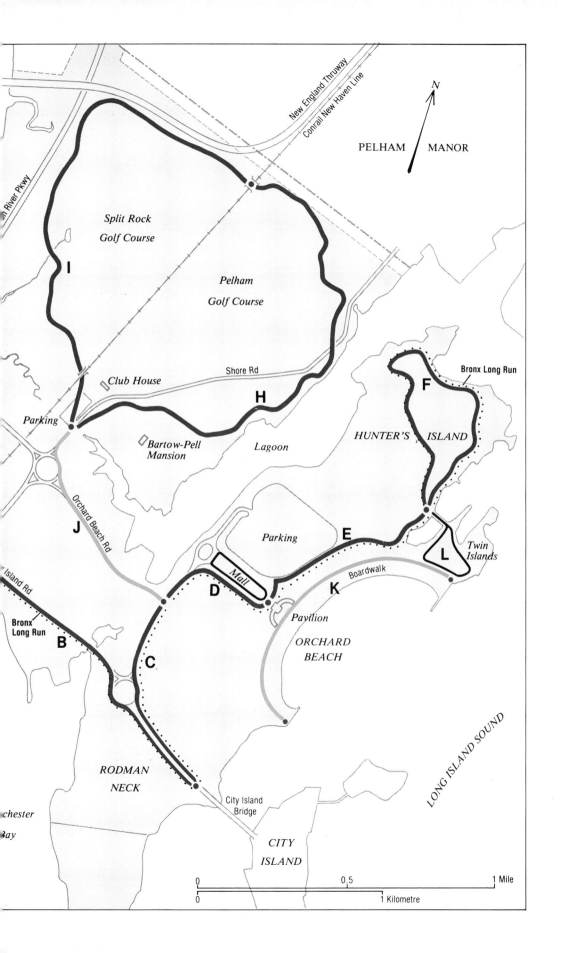

New York Botanical Garden

Bronx Long Run

Mosholu Pkwy

3 mi

Mosholu
Pkwy

Twin Lakes

Allerton Ave

Bedford Park Blvd

Webster Ave

Station

Museum
Building

Mosholu
Gate
70

Bronx River

55

110

Hemlock
Forest

Bronx Long Run

Conrail Harlem Line

Conservatory

95

105

Bronx River Pkwy

FORDHAM
UNIVERSITY

Southern Blvd

Main Gate

105

60

Snuff Mill

60

105

35

2 mi

N

E Fordham Rd

105

1 mi

55

Pelham Pkwy

Pelham and
Bronx Gate

110 Elevations in feet

Bronx Long Run

River Gate

BRONX ZOO

0   0.5 Mile

0   0.8 Kilometre

NEW YORK BOTANICAL GARDEN

3.5 miles

In just eighty-eight years, on just two hundred and fifty acres of the Bronx, a wondrous variety of plant environments and landscape moods has been assembled. The New York Botanical Garden is a delightful place to run through, and the many runners whose training garden it is lead charmed running lives. Changes in flora mark the miles. Mile 1 is Pine Hill (fifty species, alpine fragrance), Mile 2 comes at the lilac grove, and 2.5 miles brings azaleas and the forty-acre virgin (untouched since Indian days, only such virgin in New York City) Hemlock Forest. There is a Cherry Valley, a Magnolia Dell, the Bronx River to run beside, and a stone bridge to run under. The rolling hills and meandering paths of the garden make for a moderately challenging but not strenuous outing, and the successively changing plant scenery piques the runner's curiosity to go on, discover more. The Botanical Garden is a year-round pleasure and hard to top for the running of the senses—particularly during the explosive spring showoff of blooms: flashy azaleas, banks of lilacs, Daffodil Hill, violet carpets, and so forth. The heavily scented air overwhelms what little pollution may try to cross the fenceline. Along with quietly colorful runners, saffron-robed Buddhist monks can sometimes be found strolling the garden. A lovely, quiet, spirit-enriching place for running that is open daily, eight until seven in summer, ten until five in winter.

FOOTING: Mostly smooth asphalt pathways; grass and dirt trails around Twin Lakes; five good hills, some lesser inclines, one set of steps.

COURSE DIRECTIONS: Enter at Mosholu Gate (pick up map of the garden at gatehouse) and take road to right; continue past the conservatory and main gate to Pine Hill; continue to River Gate at the Bronx River; go left and follow path along west bank of river; pass under stone bridge; go left and cross the bridge near the Snuff Mill; cut right, across a parking lot, to the Pelham Gate; go left and then right past the lilacs, Cherry Valley, the day lilies; run down and then up a stiff grade (hemlocks to left), to azaleas, beeches, and magnolias; cross the Bronx River again; go right on path around the Twin Lakes; right onto asphalt roadway and back to gatehouse.

HAZARDS: Watch out for the cars; parts of the run are through fairly secluded areas, and women should run with partners to be safe.

COMFORTS: Rest rooms in the Museum Building, the Watson Building, Snuff Mill, the Conservatory, and inside the gateway at Southern Boulevard. Water fountains throughout.

MASS TRANSPORT: By railroad, take the Conrail Harlem Division to the Botanical Garden stop. By subway, take the I.R.T. Seventh Avenue No. 2 to Pelham Parkway and White Plains Road, or the Lexington Avenue I.R.T. No. 5 to Pelham Parkway and White Plains Road, or the Lexington Avenue I.R.T. No. 4 to Jerome Avenue and Fordham Road; or the I.N.D. D train to Bedford Park Boulevard and the Concourse. Parking in the garden, $2.

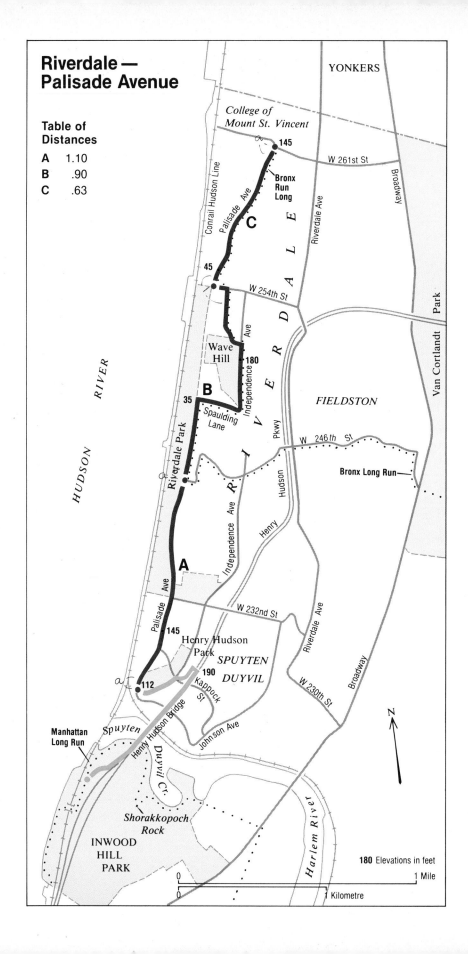

Riverdale — Palisade Avenue

Table of Distances

A	1.10
B	.90
C	.63

YONKERS

College of Mount St. Vincent

145

W 261st St

Bronx Run Long

Conrail Hudson Line

Palisade Ave

C

Broadway

Riverdale Ave

45

W 254th St

Ave

Wave Hill

180

Independence

V E R D A L E

35

B

FIELDSTON

Spaulding Lane

Pkwy

W 246th St

Hudson

R I

Bronx Long Run

Independence Ave

Henry

Van Cortlandt Park

HUDSON RIVER

Riverdale Park

A

Palisade Ave

W 232nd St

Riverdale Ave

145

Henry Hudson Park

SPUYTEN

190

DUYVIL

Kappock St

Broadway

W 230th St

112

Manhattan Long Run

Spuyten

Henry Hudson Bridge

Johnson Ave

N

Duyvil Cr.

Shorakkopoch Rock

Harlem River

INWOOD HILL PARK

180 Elevations in feet

0	1 Mile
0	1 Kilometre

RIVERDALE–PALISADE AVENUE

2.63 miles

This might be described as a rich man's run—it has everything: hills, dales, a mighty river, a small stream, ravines, estates, mansions, slate-roofed cottages, the Palisades. The Palisade Avenue route is a run down a charming country lane and is popular with the people who live along it. The scenery is gentle, the distance moderate, but the terrain is tough, with enough undulations to make you suspect you might be running the spine of a large dragon. As distraction from your quad work, concentrate on the birds, wild berries, woods and wildflowers, and the aerobically delicious air. Should you want to run a .25-mile bushwhack, a trail through the woods at the north end of Riverdale Park leaves Palisade Avenue just west of the Riverdale Country School and rejoins Palisade at 254th Street via an opening in a fence where the trail is partially blocked by a huge fallen tree trunk. (This dirt trail is best for running during spring and fall dry spells. In summer, it overgrows in the jungle syndrome.) Otherwise, turn right up Spaulding Lane, a small hill that approaches the vertical, veers left, and becomes Independence Avenue, past the Wave Hill Center for Environmental Studies. Proceed on to the Hansel and Gretel block of Sycamore Avenue, where potholes lie in front of manor houses, and where hollyhocks, arbors, and orchards surround quaint cottages. Palisade then wanders north past Arturo Toscanini's old estate, some modern glass boxes, wooded private lanes, some Victorian gingerbreads, to West 261st, the border of the College of Mount St. Vincent.

FOOTING: Variegated asphalt roadway, exceedingly well potholed in places but easily negotiable. Because the terrain includes the last toes and bunions of the worn down foothills of the Berkshires, it is quite hilly.

COURSE DIRECTIONS: After crossing the .7-mile Henry Hudson Bridge on the lower pedestrian walkway, take the first exit left and go down a flight of stairs; go left on the Henry Hudson Parkway service road and left down the less steep hill of Independence Avenue and right onto Palisade Avenue (A).

Continue 1.2 miles north on Palisade to the Riverdale Country School; right on Spaulding Lane (no sign, but recognizable by its steep pitch); left at top onto Independence Avenue; left after Wave Hill onto West 252nd, which curves downhill and jogs right to become Sycamore Avenue; left onto West 254th Street (B); immediate right to pick up Palisade Avenue again; continue north to the College of Mount St. Vincent border at West 261st Street (C). From the bottom of Spaulding Lane to West 261st Street is a hilly 1.4 miles.

HAZARDS: Few: occasional dilatory cars or motorcycles; one low section of road, near the Hayden House Apartments, that floods after heavy rains; occasional dogs guarding home turf; O.K. for night runs, but women should not run here unless accompanied by man or beast at night.

MASS TRANSPORT: Mid-Manhattan–Riverdale express bus (call 881-1000 for schedule); Conrail Hudson Line to Riverdale station at West 254th or to the Spuyten Duyvil stop at Edsall Avenue (call 532-4900 for schedule); I.R.T. Seventh Avenue No. 1 train to West 231st Street or I.N.D. Eighth Avenue A train to 207th Street and walk west.

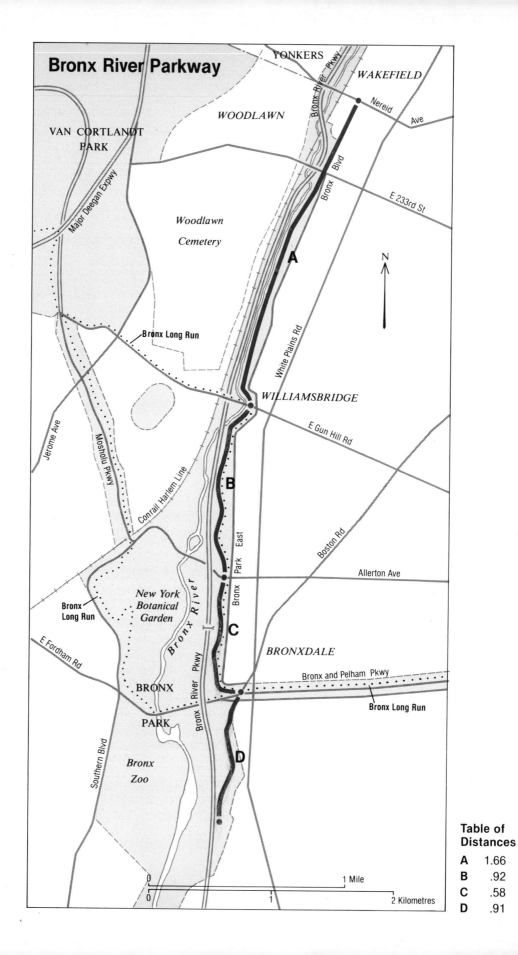

Bronx River Parkway

YONKERS

WAKEFIELD

WOODLAWN

Bronx River Pkwy

Nereid Ave

VAN CORTLANDT PARK

Major Deegan Expwy

Bronx Blvd

E 233rd St

Woodlawn Cemetery

A

N

Bronx Long Run

White Plains Rd

WILLIAMSBRIDGE

Jerome Ave

Mosholu Pkwy

Conrail Harlem Line

E Gun Hill Rd

B

Boston Rd

Bronx Park East

Allerton Ave

New York Botanical Garden

Bronx River

Bronx Long Run

C

BRONXDALE

E Fordham Rd

BRONX

Bronx River Pkwy

Bronx and Pelham Pkwy

Bronx Long Run

PARK

Southern Blvd

Bronx Zoo

D

0   1 Mile

0   1   2 Kilometres

Table of Distances

A	1.66
B	.92
C	.58
D	.91

BRONX RIVER PARKWAY

4 miles

Here you run on a strip of greensward beside what remains of the Bronx River through occasional snippets of forest, interrupted too frequently by major Parkway crossings: the Mosholu and the Bronx and Pelham. Keep in mind Moses, New York's Robert Moses, who brought together the city's parks and freeways in a bifocal mix called "parkways." The idea was to make the automobile as much an acceptable part of the natural scenery as trees and streams and grass. Thanks to Moses, one can run beside streams of traffic as well as the Bronx stream. By summer, the willows weeping over the river lend a pleasing and green visual roadblock, though it is hard not to hear the constant passing of cars. And the Bronx River, like the southern part of the borough, occasionally gets unruly, rising to a great height above her normally tame, trashed banks, and doing some damage. (The Bronx River Restoration Project is working to bring back the Bronx River, New York City's only true river in that it has its own water source. The 10-year project includes plans for a 20-mile riverside scenic walkway from the East River north to White Plains. The route will then become the Bronx River Parkway Long Run.) In all, the Bronx River Run is pleasant, uncrowded, and restful and is on the route east to Pelham Bay Park, or west to the New York Botanical Garden and Van Cortlandt Park.

FOOTING: Soft and weathered blacktop; occasional silt deposits from overflow or erosion; occasional shatterings of glass; three gentle upgrades between Gun Hill Road and Bronx Park headquarters.

COURSE DIRECTIONS: At Nereid Avenue, head south on the western sidewalk of Bronx Boulevard; go right on asphalt path at East 233rd Street, and downhill to river; left and continue south beside river, passing under Gun Hill Road (A); continue south, crossing (on crosswalk) the Mosholu (B) and the Bronx and Pelham Parkways (C); at Bronx Park headquarters (D) the path peters out; retrace to Nereid Avenue.

HAZARDS: At crosswalks for the Mosholu and the Bronx and Pelham Parkways, watch out for cars making turns—look in all directions; unleashed dogs, especially German shepherds; mud slicks on path following heavy rains; serious flooding obliterates the path at times. The 2.5 miles between Nereid Avenue and Mosholu Parkway catch enough light from the sodium-vapor lamps on the Parkway and on Bronx Boulevard to allow decent night running; at all hours it would be safest for women to run with partners (or large dogs).

COMFORTS: Few: most of the water fountains do not work; rest rooms near playground south of East 233rd Street are usually locked.

MASS TRANSPORT: I.R.T. Seventh Avenue No. 2 train to 238th Street and White Plains Road and walk four blocks west on Nereid Avenue to Bronx Boulevard, then south; No. 16 bus to Nereid Avenue and Bronx Boulevard; street parking available.

THE BRONX MINI-RUNS:

JEROME PARK RESERVOIR: Jerome Park has been reduced from what was a race track a hundred years ago to a green the size of a thin ribbon, while the 1906 reservoir takes up the other ninety-four acres. So, also, the runner is reduced to running the 2.1-mile circuit on a narrow dirt track between the cyclone fence that protects the reservoir and the heavily traveled Sedgwick, Goulden, and Reservoir Avenues. What with idling buses and constant car traffic, the route is too polluted to recommend on other than windy days, or around 5 to 6 A.M. on Sundays. Also, certain spots along the way are favored beer-drinking spas for the nearby high school and Lehman College students, who mark their festivities together by merrily breaking bottles. Watch out for glass talus and scree as well as for dog droppings. The Jerome Park track has one gentle hill, but is otherwise flat and without street crossings. It is only occasionally paved in concrete. Convenient and much used by neighborhood runners. At the junction of Sedgwick and Dickinson Avenues a one-block run on Dickinson will put you in the south-central sector of Van Cortlandt Park, and *that's* the place for running.

WOODLAWN CEMETERY: It's there, some neighborhood runners do run it, but perhaps you wouldn't want to. Almost the entire 3.5 miles is along heavily traveled roads, and the carbon monoxide is pervasive. The route is a favorite for bottle-breakers. It's also fairly deserted and not for the lone runner. The part of the route along Jerome Avenue and East 233rd Street is on concrete sidewalk, with pleasant views into the cemetery; the length of Webster Avenue is wild and weedy and flagstone-paved. The footing is so uneven as to be treacherous, and you run below—cemetery-level beside a thirty-foot-high stone wall. At East Gun Hill Road, you turn right up the hill and right again on Hull, regaining the perimeter of the cemetery with a left onto East 211th Street. This run is not recommended for lungs or bones, and should not be done unaccompanied or at night. Instead, you might follow Webster Avenue south from Gun Hill Road for four blocks and run your 3.5 miles around the New York Botanical Garden, or cross into Van Cortlandt Park at East 233rd Street and Jerome Avenue and pick up the Croton Aqueduct Run.

SPUYTEN DUYVIL LOOP: Off Palisade Avenue beneath the Henry Hudson Bridge is hidden a .85-mile running loop called Edsall Avenue, which passes the front door of the Spuyten Duyvil train station. The Edsall Avenue Run gives an opportunity to inspect from near river-level the outstanding engineering feats of the area: the Henry Hudson Bridge and the railroad swivel bridge where Spuyten Duyvil Creek meets the Hudson. The road surface is aged and corroding asphalt, and the return portion of the loop up Edsall to Palisade and Independence Avenues is all fairly steep hillwork.

FERRY POINT PARK: Ferry Point is an isolated and desolate shorefront park in which are planted the Bronx-based stanchions of the Whitestone

Bridge. A .5-mile asphalt path follows the shoreline south from the bridge. The path is severely eroded in places. The breeze off Long Island Sound is fairly stiff. Ferry Point is one of those underdone places that mapmakers color green and cities label "park." It can be reached by car or by a long run beside expressways. It's there, and runnable, but getting there does not seem worth the effort. No working facilities.

THROGS NECK: For the fifteen or so runners in this neck of the Throgs there is a challenging two-loop (connected) course with divagations. Caution! Most of these runs are through private or restricted-access properties, though runners seem to be able to pass unimpeded. Loop 1 starts at a gate to the New York Maritime College and follows the shoreline for 1.4 miles to end at the other gate to the college. There is little shade (no facilities), but there are plenty of head-turning views. A .1-mile skip gets you to the second loop.

Loop 2, a 1.5-mile circle, is run partly on the streets of Throgs Neck—Pennyfield and Schurz Avenues—and partly through the paths of Silver Beach, a private residential community. The neighborhood reminds you of small Fire Island enclaves with charming cottages, now winterized for year-round living. Runners pass through front yards on paths clearly labeled for pedestrians only.

Find someone who regularly trains on these loops to accompany you and show you the way. Local runners often meet at the fishing pier near the end of Throgs Neck Boulevard for a Sunday morning jaunt. There are some surprisingly tough little hills here. Running swimmers might like to get in a few strokes in the waters off Silver Beach, post run. Throgs Neck is somewhat cut off from the rest of the Bronx, unless you make a special trip or drive.

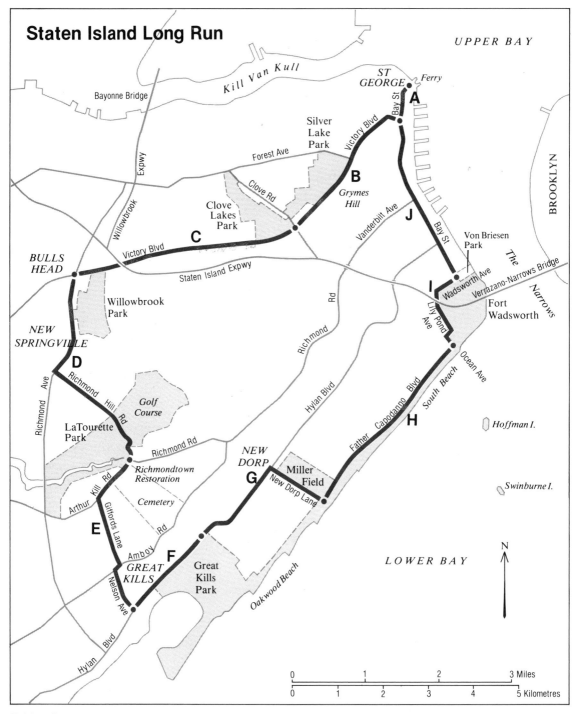

Staten Island Long Run

UPPER BAY

Kill Van Kull

Bayonne Bridge

ST GEORGE
Ferry

A

Silver Lake Park

Forest Ave

Victory Blvd

Bay St

Clove Rd

B

Grymes Hill

J

Expwy

Willowbrook

Clove Lakes Park

Vanderbilt Ave

Bay St

BROOKLYN

C

Victory Blvd

Staten Island Expwy

Rd

Von Briesen Park

Wadsworth Ave

Verrazano-Narrows Bridge

The Narrows

BULLS HEAD

I

Fort Wadsworth

Willowbrook Park

Richmond

Lily Pond Ave

NEW SPRINGVILLE

D

Richmond Ave

Richmond Hill Rd

Golf Course

Hylan Blvd

Ocean Ave

Father Capodanno Blvd

South Beach

H

Hoffman I.

LaTourette Park

Richmond Rd

NEW DORP

Miller Field

Swinburne I.

Arthur Kill Rd

Richmondtown Restoration

G

New Dorp Lane

E

Giffords Lane

Cemetery

Rd

N

F

Amboy

GREAT KILLS

Great Kills Park

LOWER BAY

Nelson Ave

Hylan Blvd

Oakwood Beach

0   1   2   3 Miles

0   1   2   3   4   5 Kilometres

Table of Distances

A	.60	F	1.37
B	2.15	G	2.31
C	3.20	H	2.71
D	3.60	I	1.20
E	2.42	J	2.36

STATEN ISLAND

Most any five-borough runner, up against the wall and pressed for the three words that characterize Staten Island running, would without hesitation utter the expletives "Hilly! Hillier! Hilliest!" If it's hard to find a hill in Queens, it's hard *not* to find one on Staten Island. Some runners, in search of perpetual resistance, move to Staten Island just for its hills, the six biggest being Todt, Emerson, Grymes, Lighthouse, Ward, and Fort. Staten Islanders tend to smile tolerantly when told of demon hills elsewhere in the city. Central Park's Great Hill is a cakewalk for them, and the annual Stapleton Steeplechase is the course they'll invite you to try for some "real hills." Given hills as steep as Hillside Avenue—Hillside runners are considered to be in a serious training condition—or Snake Hill, a legendary sidewinder, or the Richmond Hill Road switchback behind the Richmondtown Restoration, or the mile-long, three-bump endurance fight up Victory Boulevard between Bay Street and Silver Lake Park—you are guaranteed challenging resistance running almost any place you choose to set foot on the island. (Hill-phobic runners should avoid Staten Island and plead quaditis if necessary.) In fact, the first mile of the New York City Marathon is all uphill from Staten Island on the Verrazano-Narrows Bridge.

Staten Island's other prime offering is nearly seven miles of beach running on the sands of South Beach, Midland Beach, New Dorp Beach, and Oakwood Beach, and in Great Kills Park out to Crookes Point. If you hanker for a week on Cape Cod but can only manage a day on Staten Island, you may be surprised at how nicely Staten Island will do.

Another kind of running special to Staten Island and not possible in the other boroughs is country-road running. The best place to try it is off Hylan Boulevard, in the area south of Great Kills. (Frederick Law Olmsted once had a farm in this vicinity.) Hylan is crosshatched by country lanes, east-west. Here it is possible to run for miles in a country setting, or at least a subsuburban one, seeing few cars or people. This remoteness has both advantages and disadvantages. Much of the southern, Tottenville, portion of Staten Island strikes one as *Deliverance* country and not particularly safe for the lone runner, especially the lone woman runner. Also, here in the city, the country comes with a poisonous overburden—the chemical-laced breezes that blow to southern and western Staten Island from New Jersey.

Still, Staten Island—usually thought of as that other borough, or the borough manqué, or part of New Jersey—has the most bucolic of treats for the New York City runner who is willing to work for them. The disjointed moods of the island have to do with the haphazard way it is developing—sprawling, really. You will run a charming stretch of eighteenth- and nineteenth-century small-town America (where the annual Flag Day Parade is a neighborhood event, and the folks turn out on their porches to wave little American flags), and then you'll run a stretch of the most garish late-twentieth-century malled and tract-ravaged land. And most Staten Islanders, even the runners, are car-dependent. Staten Island is predominantly a white, working-class conservative community, where everyone drives, few walk, and the male athletes go off to college, major in phys. ed., and come straight back to Staten Island to coach at the old high school.

Staten Island runners, as well as being insular, are cluster runners, whose primary cluster is in Clove Lakes Park. Most of them run, most of the time, in this small area and leave the exotic distance explorations to off-islanders. (The native runners wear baseball caps and talk fast; the outsiders wear T-shirts from other boroughs, other races.)

Staten Island is the city's only running space to be approached by ferry. Once landed in St. George, you know you have come to a very different city place. Staten Island does not look like New York, nor does it feel like New York, but the spectacular sky-ridge cross-harbor is Manhattan's, and confirms the proximity. The 22.5-mile Staten Island Long Run begins and ends at St. George—allowing both warmup and warmdown on the Staten Island Ferry—and offers a full salad, mixing hill running, lake running, town-and-country running, beach running, with a pause, midway, in earliest Colonial America. The Richmondtown Restoration deserves a stop and a sniff—in the 1695 little red Voorlezer's House, the oldest known elementary school in the country, and in the General Store, the smithy, the cooper's, and the basket-maker's. Staten Island runs you back through seventeenth-century village America, then runs you past the contemporary scene and the run turns nostalgic. On Staten Island, the Long Run is a treasure hunt on which you keep hoping to glimpse more pieces of the solid past just down the road beyond the next shopping mall. Sometimes you do.

CLOVE LAKES PARK

2.91 miles, flat course
2.87 miles, hill course

Of the Staten Islanders who run, ninety percent of them run Clove Lakes, and most Staten Island running, organized and disorganized, takes place here—despite the fact that the paths are narrow and the hills are steep. A wooded, linear park in the northern interior of Staten Island, Clove Lakes can be run entirely on the flats, twice around two of its pond-sized lakes —Clove and Martling—for 2.91 miles (which the natives call 3; you will most likely set your personal record for the 3). Or you can add Brook's Lake on steep hill paths, for an additional 2.87 miles. This strenuous resistance route, Staten Island's Grand Prix, has been the traditional testing ground for the island's high-school cross-country teams since the 1930's. The Hill Course passes through some of the city's prime mulberry orchards, and it is probable that in the month of June mulberrying will interrupt your running, unless you are an extremely disciplined carbohydrate loader.

If the identifying mark of the Staten Island runner is a baseball cap, the running club of reckoning is the Staten Island Athletic Club, under the presidency of Bob Orazem. The club organizes races in the park throughout the year—many open only to Staten Island residents—and sponsors 10 A.M. Saturday fun runs (.5 mile for kids under ten, the Clove Lakes "3 Miles" for everyone else), preceded by starting-line mini-clinics and followed by the awarding of finishing certificates and prizes that range from oranges to pineapples to locust swatters, fifty-two weekends a year. The weekly fun run results are carried in the *Staten Island Advance*. The annual Thanksgiving race,three miles and only for islanders, is about to enter its fourth decade.

Staten Island nonrunners are also partial to Clove Lakes, and teen-agers treat it like a Class-A summer hangout. They may make sideline comments on your exertions but, unlike kids in Brooklyn, never ask if they can run "witch youse." Taken together, the runners and the nonrunners make for a sizable summer throng. Staten Island's most popular course is best run in the crepuscule—A.M. or P.M.

FOOTING: Generally smooth asphalt paths, except after rains when mud overruns the trails at low spots; it is possible to run on the grass beside the asphalt. Or you could run the bridle path, but locals don't, owing to heavy horse traffic.

COURSE DIRECTIONS: Flat Course: Begin on the parking-lot side of the boathouse off Clove Road and head northwest on the asphalt path between the lake and the bridle path; left over bridge; right after bridge; right over small wood bridge before Martling Lake; left at Martling Avenue (A), cross bridge and left onto path around the other side of the lake; continue straight until the boathouse bridge (B); left onto the bridge and repeat the course (A + B), for 2.91 miles on the flats.

Hill Course: Same start as Flat Course, but at Martling Avenue (A) cross Martling and continue northwest on an asphalt path that leads to Forest Avenue; go left on Forest and cross a small bridge; go left on path after bridge and continue beside a small stream back to Martling Avenue (C); cross Martling at Slosson and head uphill, keeping to the farthest right path; pass firehouse and continue uphill; go left at second triangle of paths; cross bridle path; drop downhill; take first right and follow path almost to Victory Boulevard; go left and downhill; left before ice-skating rink; return to boathouse (D).

HAZARDS: Kids on bicycles; fishhooks on the fly; muddy footing near Martling Lake after rains; untended dogs; horses; crowds of strollers on weekends and summer afternoons (best run early morning or early evening); except for the stretch around Martling Avenue, where the winter winds are harsh, Clove Lakes is protected by its hills and is relatively free from the high winds that often buffet other sections of Staten Island; women should not run alone in the isolated areas of this park (muggings, stabbings, and murder have occurred here in recent years); no night running, because of poor lighting.

COMFORTS: Rest rooms, fountains, and refreshments at park headquarters and at boathouse, where there is a summer restaurant. Very shady.

MASS TRANSPORT: Staten Island Ferry to St. George; R6, R7, R106, R107, R110, or R112 bus.

EXTENSIONS: 1) .9-mile run up Victory Boulevard to Silver Lake Park (E). 2) Clove Lakes is at the 2.5-mile point in the 22.5-mile Staten Island Long Run.

CLOVES LAKES PARK—MEASURED COURSES

3 miles	(A + B) x 2	**plus** .1 mile
3 miles	D + C	**plus** .01 mile
4 miles	D + C + A + D	minus .08 mile
5 miles	A + B + A + C + D + A	minus .04 mile
6 miles	D + C + B + D + C + B + A	minus .08 mile
8 miles	D + C + B + D + C + B + A + D + C	minus .07 mile
10 miles	D + C + B + D + C + B + A + D + C + (B x 3)	minus .02 mile

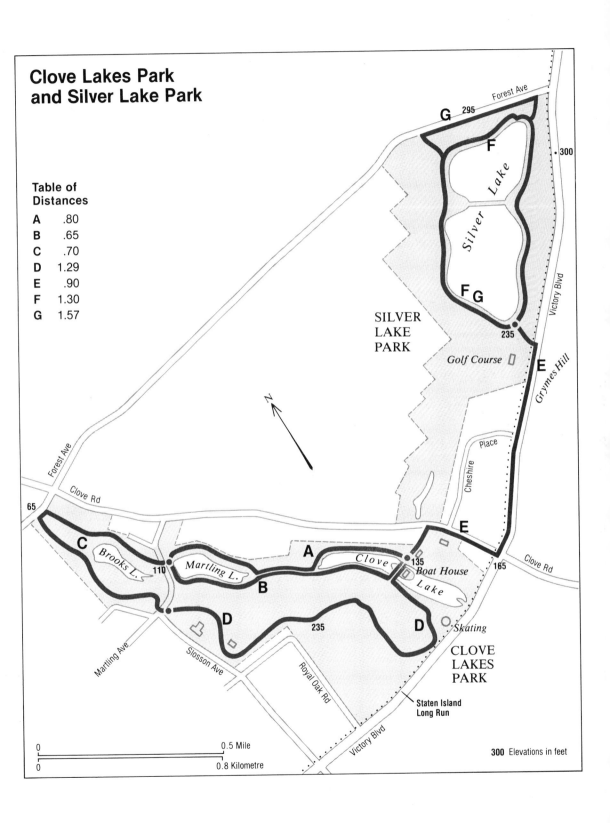

Clove Lakes Park
and Silver Lake Park

Table of Distances

A	.80
B	.65
C	.70
D	1.29
E	.90
F	1.30
G	1.57

G 295

F

300

Silver Lake

SILVER LAKE PARK

F G

235

Golf Course

E

Grymes Hill

Victory Blvd

Forest Ave

Forest Ave

Clove Rd

65

C

Brooks L.

110

Martling L.

B

A

Clove

135

Boat House

Lake

165

Clove Rd

E

Cheshire Place

D

235

D

Skating

CLOVE LAKES PARK

Martling Ave

Slosson Ave

Royal Oak Rd

Victory Blvd

Staten Island Long Run

N

0   0.5 Mile

0   0.8 Kilometre

300 Elevations in feet

SILVER LAKE

1.3 miles, lower loop
1.57 miles, hill loop

Though connected to Clove Lakes along the umbilical of Victory Boulevard, Silver Lake is less known and less favored by the mass of Staten Island runners. Silver Lake provides top-of-Staten Island running around a reservoir, beside the greens of golf course and tree, and in almost too much fragrance of honeysuckle and roses in summer. Dependably breezy for enjoyable summer running even on hot days, and when the chemical smog disperses there is a view to New Jersey—Bayonne and Elizabeth. Silver Lake is used mainly by Staten Island's serious distance racers, like Art Hall, president of the North Shore A.C., for obvious reasons: "There's no one here, no recreation, no concessions, no horses, no fishing; it's never crowded. You can run in this park and worry about nothin' but your feet."

In the modestly rarified running atmosphere of Silver Lake you have a choice of doing the flats only or adding a big hill each time around, where you might catch a few of New York's top runners on their regular training runs. There is a marked mile, quartered, in yellow paint on the reservoir path, which begins off Silver Lake Park Road below Forest Avenue. Silver Lake is only .9 mile uproad from the crowds of Clove Lakes, and only a 1.5-mile *stiff* hill-upon-hill run up from the Staten Island Ferry.

FOOTING: Excellent, smooth asphalt; one set of steps on the lower loop; a short stretch of concrete sidewalk with a sprinkling of broken glass beside Forest Avenue on the hill loop.

COURSE DIRECTIONS: Pick up Silver Lake Park Road just past the golf-club parking lot off Victory Boulevard; turn right onto asphalt path that feeds into reservoir loop path to join the run counter-clockwise. For the flat course (F), keep to the reservoir fence. For the hill course (G), just past the 1-mile mark on the pavement take the asphalt path going right and uphill to Forest Avenue; left on sidewalk beside Forest Avenue; left on Silver Lake Park Road (where marked mile begins); pick up the reservoir fence again.

HAZARDS: Luxuriant poison ivy climbing the chain link fence around the reservoir and fingering onto the running path in summer; an exposed hilltop with little useful shade by the path, beware the sun; free-blown (and bitter) wind zone in winter; gangs of kids congregate here on nice summer evenings; well lighted and considered safe for night running, though women are advised to run with partners; occasional muggers; occasional rapists.

COMFORTS: Few: Most of the water fountains do not work. No rest rooms.

MASS TRANSPORT: Staten Island Ferry to St. George; R6, R7, R106, R111, or R112 bus.

EXTENSIONS: 1) .9-mile jaunt down Victory Boulevard to Clove Lakes Park. 2) Silver Lake sits at the 1.5-mile mark of the 22.5-mile Staten Island Long Run.

GREAT KILLS PARK

5 miles

Urban dune running in a national park, part of the Gateway National Recreation Area. Most of the run is behind the dunes on flat sand and dirt paths, with occasional patches of asphalt, though a beach run along the tide line can be added, or substituted. The course is the most comfortable, least strenuous that Staten Island has to offer and is not much used for running. In the summer of 1978, a couple of races were run in Great Kills, fairly informal affairs; but road racing seems to have been a thing of one season here, and most Staten Island racing remains at Clove Lakes.

The 1.75-mile beach run out to Crookes Point is best done at low tide to take advantage of the firm sand at the water's edge. The back acreage at Great Kills includes a 440-yard track, more sand than cinder at this point, but open to the public.

The scenery here is not unlike that of Cape Cod—same sea birds, same sea breezes, same sweet ocean air, and not a hill in sight for foot. The swing past Great Kills Harbor offers the sway of masts over sea grass. The presence of uniformed National Park mounties adds an unexpected and picturesque element to the scene and places it far beyond the city's borders. When your resistance is down and you want only flats, Great Kills is a pleasant running spa.

FOOTING: Firmly packed dirt and gravel road; some soft asphalt pathway; beach sand; absolutely flat. No bumps at all.

COURSE DIRECTIONS: Begin at Hylan Boulevard on asphalt path to left of Great Kills entry road; continue past administration building (A); turn left onto dirt road; continue on road out to Crookes Point bulkhead (B); turn around and retrace the road to administration parking lot (B); there take road to left; skirt harbor; at road fork, turn right; skirt old cinder track and turn right following sand road out to Hylan Boulevard (C).

OTHER RUNS: 1) 1.75-mile sprint along the Great Kills beach (D). 2) 440-yard cinder-and-sand track, neglected and weedy.

HAZARDS: Cars and motorbikes on road portion of run and dust kicked up by such vehicles; strong sun and no shade; grass fires in spring and fall—don't attempt to run through even a small wall of flame.

COMFORTS: Rest rooms throughout the park in the form of portable outhouses, and federal water fountains that work!

MASS TRANSPORT: Staten Island Ferry to St. George. R103 bus to Hylan Boulevard and Great Kills entrance.

EXTENSIONS: 1) Go north on Hylan Boulevard a few blocks, then bushwhack right through the area behind Oakwood Beach, which was flattened by a hurricane some years ago, to the Oakwood Beach end of the South Beach Run. 2) Alternatively, go north on Hylan Boulevard for 1.39 miles to New Dorp Lane. Turn right onto New Dorp Lane and run beside Miller Field till you connect with the South Beach Run.

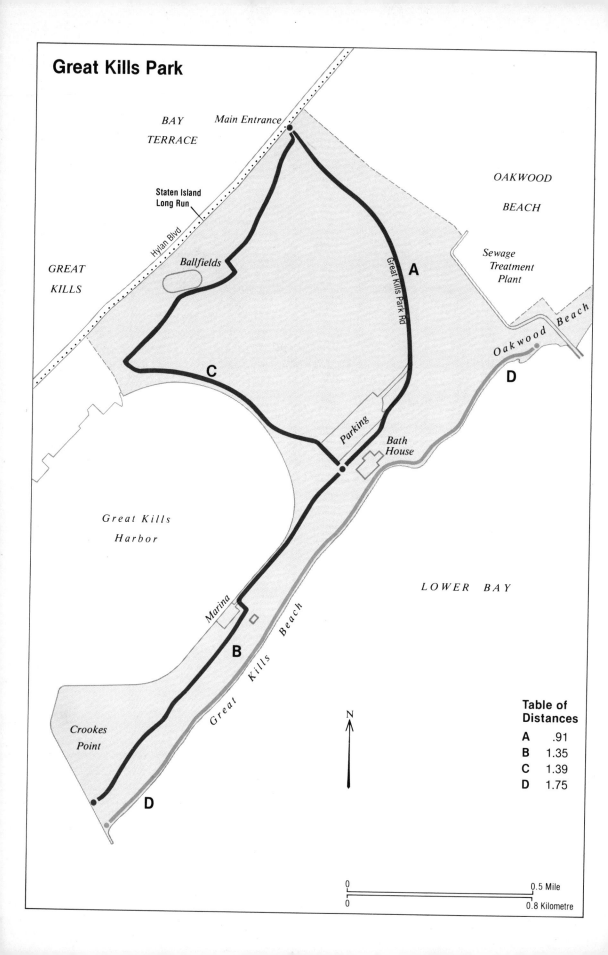

South Beach— Oakwood Beach

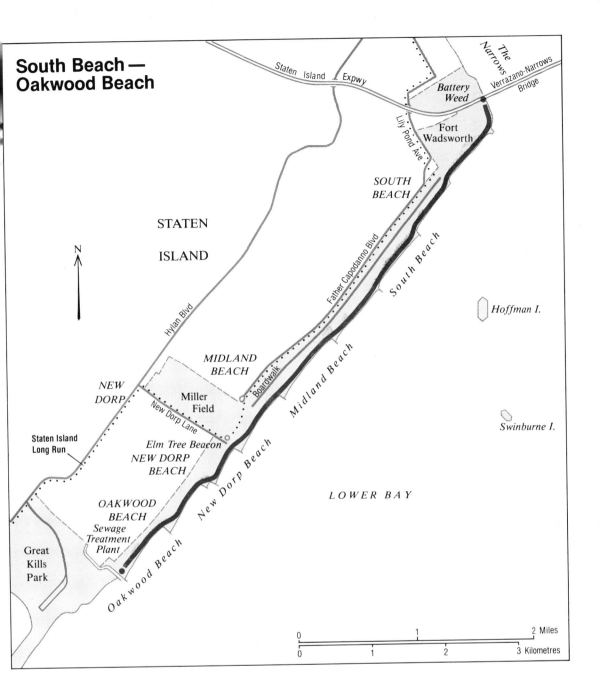

STATEN ISLAND Expwy

Battery Weed

The Narrows

Verrazano-Narrows Bridge

Lily Pond Ave

Fort Wadsworth

SOUTH BEACH

STATEN

ISLAND

N

South Beach

Father Capodanno Blvd

Hoffman I.

Hylan Blvd

MIDLAND BEACH

Boardwalk

Midland Beach

Swinburne I.

NEW DORP

Miller Field

New Dorp Lane

Elm Tree Beacon

NEW DORP BEACH

New Dorp Beach

LOWER BAY

Staten Island Long Run

OAKWOOD BEACH

Sewage Treatment Plant

Great Kills Park

Oakwood Beach

0   1   2 Miles

0   1   2   3 Kilometres

SOUTH BEACH—OAKWOOD BEACH

5 miles

This beach run, on sand, is along one of the great open spaces in New York City. It is part of the Gateway National Recreation Area, though not much recreated. South is the first of four adjacent beaches (Midland, New Dorp, Oakwood), and the run ends at an impassable sewage creek that marks the northern border of Great Kills Park. If you are comfortable on sand and have an affinity for the minus heel, you can enjoy simply paralleling the horizon, racing sandpipers, sprinting beside waves—past fishermen and dunes and dilapidated old beach shacks. The longest beach run on Staten Island, South Beach is recommended in particular for sunrise and sunset runs, or for times (consult shipping schedules in paper) when the big ships sail under the Verrazano. The south-north run offers awesome views, under the Verrazano-Narrows Bridge, of a pinhead Manhattan, of Brooklyn, out to sea, toward Europe. Worth running for the fresh air and the quiet.

FOOTING: Firmly packed sand at water's edge, gentle and good to the foot, provided you don't have a podiatric problem—knee, back, or Achilles tendon—that makes sand a strain; best run at or near low tide for firmest footing (check newspaper tide charts); a few rock bulkheads that must be scrambled over, possibility of scraping hands and knees; when running at sea level remember that the beach itself slopes seaward and that, better than running the full distance with the seaward hip lower than the landward, it would be preferable to repeat part of the route in the opposite direction.

COURSE DIRECTIONS: Runner has the choice of beginning this run at Oakwood Beach and heading north for five miles to the foot of the Verrazano, watching it grow in immensity, or beginning at South Beach, first clambering over the rocks at its north end, under the Verrazano, and running away from the bridge. In either case, let the wave line be your guide.

HAZARDS: An occasional unleashed dog; an occasional glob of tar; sudden temperature drops, especially after sundown, and stiff winds (you might want to carry a windbreaker); stinging sand spray; loose, dry deep sand that can twist ankles, strain Achilles tendons; unshaded, high glare run; no barefoot running, owing to glass and seashells in sand; one-mile Roosevelt Boardwalk too dilapidated for safe running; ocean water unfit for swimming, but some inveterate beach bathers swim here nonetheless.

MASS TRANSPORT: Staten Island Ferry to St. George (warmup on the ferry); S2 bus out Seaside Boulevard to Lily Pond for South Beach, to Emmet Avenue for Oakwood Beach.

EXTENSION: A .5-mile dump-and-street run from the south end of Oakwood Beach out Emmet Avenue, left on Hylan Boulevard and left into Great Kills Park for the 5-mile Great Kills loop.

STATEN ISLAND MINI-RUNS:

WOLFE'S POND PARK: Purchased by the city in 1930 at the urging of Robert Moses, Wolfe's Pond is barely 1.5 miles around, and much of that is bushwhacking through tangles of briers and poison ivy that make the effort hardly worth the run. It is not walked or run much, except by occasional Tottenville High cross-country teams. It's quite deserted, aside from the picnic area, and the runner will be hard-pressed to keep on the right path. Skip it or bring a machete.

WILLOWBROOK PARK: There is a .5-mile run around the lake and a somewhat longer run on trails through the nearby woods of Willowbrook Park, which occupies the part of Staten Island once known as the Great Swamp. Willowbrook is a red-hot softball center, but it's as flat and as dreary a little park as you will find. Next door is the infamous institution for the retarded that formerly bore the same name. The only reason for looping this place is happenstance, if you are passing by on a connecting leg of the 22.5-mile Staten Island Long Run.

STAPLETON STEEPLECHASE: Technically not a mini-run but an annual early summer Staten Island event (on the same day as eight other events, of lesser distance) of ten miles on roads and hills around Stapleton, one of the island's oldest neighborhoods. The course includes Staten Island's killer, Hillside Avenue, a .25-mile upper on cobblestones, plus many other bumps and hillocks. A tough course, but fun because of the people. (For information and map write The Mud Lane Society, P.O. Box 174, Staten Island, N.Y. 10304.)

A. VON BRIESEN PARK: This park contains a .42-mile loop, half up and half down, through a tiny, beautifully landscaped, verdant, and well-behaved park. No steps. It's worth a slight detour from the Staten Island Long Run for magnificent views of The Narrows and the Verrazano-Narrows Bridge. On the side of the park away from Fort Wadsworth you look out over an exquisite Monet-type lily pond. The small parking lot might also serve as the origin for the Staten Island Long Run. There are no facilities here, though water and rest rooms can be found at the adjacent Fort Wadsworth, if it is receiving visitors on that particular day.

LONG RUNS

The descriptions of the Long Runs listed here are already of such length that to do more than give the skeletal directions would stretch them to interminable length. Therefore, stripped of color, and pared to an essential turn-right, turn-left, a few long runs are presented that either wrap up each borough or take you out of the city altogether.

MANHATTAN LONG RUN

31 miles

Battery Park at the southern tip of Manhattan is as good a place as any to begin Ted Corbitt's 31-mile Manhattan Long Run. Head north on West Street beside the Hudson River. Run at street level or on the two remaining elevated miles of the Westside Highway. (Exit at Chambers Street from the Highway.) Go north on Eleventh Avenue to Sixtieth Street. Cross through the railroad yard to the riverside promenade of Riverside Park at Seventy-second Street (A = 6.25 miles). Continue north beside the river—at Eighty-eighth Street, the path is perilously close to traffic and single file is necessary—to the 125th Street pier. It is sometimes possible to continue north beside the river to the George Washington Bridge (B = 5.5 miles) if the gates to the sewage-treatment plant are open. Otherwise, at 132nd Street move inland one block to Twelfth Avenue. Mount the steps to Riverside Drive at 135th Street. Continue along beside the Henry Hudson Parkway north of the George Washington to a left-exit ramp before Dyckman Street. Go left and take the first left after passing under the Henry Hudson, onto Staff Street. Descend the hill and go left onto Dyckman Street and out to the river. Go right and north on the river path. Turn right and take the steps up a pedestrian bridge that crosses over railroad tracks near a roller-hockey rink. Go left and north on a trail that parallels the Henry Hudson Parkway. When the waters of the Spuyten Duyvil Creek are in sight, the trail curves right and passes under the Henry Hudson Bridge. Continue downhill to the Shorakkopoch Rock (C = 3 miles), then left out of the park along 218th Street and past Baker Field to Tenth Avenue. Go south under the elevated to the junction of Dyckman Street and the Harlem River Driveway.

Pick up the asphalt path alongside the Harlem River Driveway, west side of the road, and run south to the 125th Street (D = 6.67 miles) end point of the East River Run. (Follow Harlem River Run course directions.) Continue south beside the East River (E = 9.6 miles) to South Ferry. (Follow East River Run course directions.) You have looped Manhattan in 31 miles *in toto*.

THE BROOKLYN LONG RUN

44 miles

Begin at the Manhattan end of the Brooklyn Bridge and cross to Cadman Plaza East for 1.12 miles. Go right, through Cadman Plaza Park; go straight on Middagh to the Brooklyn Heights Promenade; run the promenade down and back and return to Cadman Plaza for 1.4 miles. Go right onto Court Street and continue south till Union; left on Union; right on Fourth Avenue (A = 4.62 miles). Go right on Sixty-seventh Street; left through Owl's Head Park; right on Sixty-ninth Street to the Sixty-ninth Street pier (B = 4.4 miles). Run beside the Shore Parkway from Bay Ridge at the Sixty-ninth Street pier to Bensonhurst for 4.32 miles. Continue south on the Shore Parkway service road over the Cropsey Avenue bridge to Coney Island at West Thirty-seventh (C = 7.02 miles). Run left and east on the Coney Island Boardwalk for 2.45 miles (D + E). Pass through Brighton Beach, Manhattan Beach, Sheepshead Bay, and out beside the Shore Parkway again and over the Marine Parkway Bridge to the west end of Jacob Riis Park at Beach 169th in Rockaway (F = 7.37 miles). Retrace route as far as the Coney Island Boardwalk and Ocean Parkway (F + E = 8.07 miles). Go right and follow Ocean Parkway (G = 5.2 miles) to Prospect Park. Turn right, enter the park and follow the Park Drive to the right to Grand Army Plaza for 1.8 miles. Go left on Union Street, cross Fourth Avenue (H = 2.55 miles), and continue on Union. Turn right on Court Street, right again and through Cadman Plaza Park, and back to the steps to the Brooklyn Bridge for the final 2.1 miles (A minus the promenade and Brooklyn Bridge). The Short Brooklyn Long Run comes to 27.6 miles by the addition of A + B + C + D + G + H + A (minus the promenade and Brooklyn Bridge on the final A leg).

QUEENS LONG RUN

20 miles

The Queens Long Run was inadvertently designed for runners by Robert Moses. Start at Flushing Meadow Park at the Taystee Bread parking lot on Avery Avenue. Go south under the Van Wyck Expressway and over a pedestrian bridge into the Queens Botanical Garden to the Main Street gate. Head diagonally left across Main Street to pick up the Colden Street bicycle path. Go right to the intersection of Rose Avenue and Kissena Boulevard. Go left on Rose Avenue to the Bowne Street entrance to Kissena Park. Go right and cross the park to Underhill Avenue. Follow Underhill Avenue southeast and cross Utopia Parkway (A = 3.4 miles), to the pedestrian crossing over the Long Island Expressway. Continue to Francis Lewis Boulevard. Turn right onto Francis Lewis Boulevard and stay on the dirt path. Go left on Seventy-third Avenue and pass under the Clearview Expressway. Turn right onto Hollis Court Boulevard to the entrance onto the

Old Motor Highway. The path is to the left before a trestle and is marked by a large sign with a bicycle on it.

Take the Old Motor Highway to the left cutoff (B = 3.6 miles)—look for arrows on the pavement—for the Alley North Run. (See course directions for the Alley North Run.) The run is all cross-country to 233rd Street and West Alley. Cross over the Long Island Expressway and take a set of stairs down to the right. Pick up the asphalt path that parallels the Cross-Island Parkway north to the Cloverdale Boulevard exit. Continue north on Cloverdale Boulevard. Go right onto Northern Boulevard, then left after the Cross-Island to pick up the bicycle-jogging path at the northeast corner of the intersection (C = 2.82 miles). This intersection is dangerous.

Head north on the path to the right of the Cross-Island Parkway. Pass Crocheron Park, en route the Bell Boulevard entrance to Fort Totten. Continue on dirt paths under the Throgs Neck Bridge and out to Utopia Parkway at Totten Street (D = 3.42 miles). Go south on Utopia Parkway to Underhill Avenue (E = 3.37 miles). Retrace the route through Kissena Park and Corridor to the Taystee Bread parking lot (A) for an out-and-back loop of 20 miles.

THE BRONX LONG RUN

24.5 miles

Begin at West 261st and Palisade Avenue. Go south on Palisade for 1.5 miles to West 246th Street. Go left and continue east on West 246th through Fieldston for 1 mile to West 242nd and Broadway at Van Cortlandt Park (A = 2.5 miles). Take path due east at 242nd and Broadway through the park to Dickinson Avenue (B = 1.24 miles). Pick up the Mosholu Parkway corridor heading southeast. Enter the New York Botanical Garden at the Mosholu Gate and go right to the River Gate. Go east from the River Gate on the Bronx and Pelham Parkway corridor, crossing the Bronx River Parkway (C = 2.8 miles), to Pelham Bay Park at Garbage Mountain (D = 2.7 miles). Go left and north on the Cahit Yeter Trail (follow the yellow arrows) past Orchard Beach, around Hunter's Island, and back to Garbage Mountain (E = 8.5 miles). Retrace the Bronx and Pelham Parkway corridor west to the Bronx River Parkway just past White Plains Road (D). Go right and continue north by the Bronx River Parkway to Gun Hill Road. Go left and continue west on Gun Hill Road to Mosholu and Dickinson Avenue (F = 2.7 miles). Retrace the path through Van Cortlandt Park from Dickinson Avenue, north and west to 242nd Street and Broadway for the final 1.24 miles (B). 24.5 miles. The Bronx all-but marathon.

STATEN ISLAND LONG RUN

22.5 miles

For most people, the Staten Island Long Run begins with a 25-cent ride on the Staten Island Ferry. Once across the harbor, leave the ferry terminal and take a left onto Bay Street. Go right onto Victory Boulevard (A = .6 mile) and up three long, steep pitches to Forest Avenue at Silver Lake Park. Continue on Victory Boulevard to Clove Road (B = 2.16 miles). Go straight on Victory Boulevard past the entrance to Willowbrook Park to Richmond Avenue (C = 3.2 miles). Turn left onto Richmond Avenue; go left onto Richmond Hill Road for a one-mile climb to the corner of LaTourette Park Golf Course. Continue a half mile to the switchback down to the Richmondtown Restoration, Richmond Hill Road at Richmond Road (D = 3.6 miles). Continue on Richmond Hill Road which becomes Arthur Kill Road, past a cemetery to Giffords Lane. Go left onto Giffords Lane, right on Amboy Road, and left on Nelson Avenue. Turn left on Hylan Boulevard (E = 2.4 miles) and run on the sidewalk to the entrance to Great Kills Park (F = 1.37 miles). Continue on Hylan to New Dorp Lane. Go right onto New Dorp and leave Miller Field to the left. Continue straight to the beach (G = 2.3 miles). Jog left to a slight rise where a dirt path leads to Father Capodanno Boulevard. Runners have a choice of staying on Capodanno or moving right to the Franklin D. Roosevelt Boardwalk or onto the beach.

Continue north to Drury Avenue and Ocean Avenue (H = 2.7 miles). Go left and make the steep ascent of Lily Pond Avenue, passing Fort Wadsworth on the right. Cross beneath the Staten Island Expressway and go right on Wadsworth. Turn left onto Bay Street (I = 1.2 miles) and continue on Bay past Victory (J = 2.35 miles) to the ferry (A). 22.5 miles all told.

PALISADES INTERSTATE PARK—GEORGE WASHINGTON BRIDGE LONG RUN

1.27 miles (George Washington Bridge)   *6-mile park loop*

Begin on the switchback ramp south of the bridge on the east side of Riverside Drive. Exit on Haven and West 177th Street. Go right on 177th, left on Cabrini Boulevard and left on West 178th Street to the pedestrian path across the south side of the bridge. Run on concrete sidewalk to the first street on the Jersey shore. Go south, down River Road hill, and take the first left onto the Henry Hudson Drive. Be extremely watchful, as there is no sidewalk here. Head down and around the hairpin curve to the flats beneath the cliffs of Fort Lee Historical Park.

Continue north on this paved road to a boat basin. Pick up a dirt path along the river's edge to the Englewood Boat Basin (and water stop). Because the sun sets behind the Palisades, the entire course can become quite dark and cold by late afternoon.

From the Englewood Boat Basin, switch back and forth across the face of the Palisades on the concrete sidewalk (.8 miles), and watch out for cars out of control. Just before meeting the Palisades Interstate Parkway, on the south side of the street, take the slate steps up to the blue-blazed Long Path into the woods. This is a rugged trail, used mainly by hikers. Go south to a covered pedestrian bridge at the southwest corner of the park, to the George Washington Bridge sidewalk. Approximately six miles on land.

THURSDAY NIGHT BRIDGE RUN

13 miles

The New York distance runner's obligatory equivalent of the politician's weekly prayer breakfast is the weekly Thursday-night-vespers run—The Bridge Run—from the door of the N.Y.R.R.C. headquarters on West Sixty-third Street to the George Washington Bridge, 13 miles out-and-back and all but the crosstown miles of it along Riverside Park. In the fair-weather months before the October New York City Marathon, this group of fast, postconversational, ultraserious distance runners grows from a manageable hard core of frostbitten regulars to several platoons, many of the once-a-year-marathon variety. The only course marker used or needed, is the George Washington Bridge.

OLD CROTON AQUEDUCT LONG RUN

11 miles

This run north out of the city into the wilderness-with-backyards of Westchester county makes an ideal New York City Marathon training route, because the course is almost flat. Much of the route is shaded, except where it passes through the grounds of estates.

To begin in Van Cortlandt Park, go east from 242nd and Broadway past the lake and golf starter's shack to the stairs for the bridge that parallels the Major Deegan Expressway and crosses over the Mosholu Parkway. Head north, cross McLean Avenue in Yonkers and continue north. The trail passes by the eastern edge of Tibbett's Brook Park. Just northeast of Tibbett's, the first big disconnect occurs, at Yonkers Avenue. Follow Yonkers Avenue left (moving in a northwesterly direction) to Oakland Cemetery. Go right onto Ashburton Avenue, which curves left and northwest. Go right on-to Broadway, and north for two blocks, then left onto Lamartine Avenue (steep downhill). The Aqueduct path, unmarked, can be rejoined on the right, just before Lamartine Terrace.

About two miles past Lamartine, at Odell Avenue in northern Yonkers, there is an "Old Croton Trailway" marker. Continue another 1.7 miles to the far side of the Hastings-on-Hudson dump where the trail crosses Farragut Parkway and Broadway. The path continues east of Broadway for a mile, then crosses to the west side of Broadway in Dobbs Ferry at Eldredge Place and Hatch Terrace. The trail goes north for another half mile to Main and Cedar Streets.

From Main Street, Dobbs Ferry, it is 3.2 mostly rustic, estate-skirting, Hudson-viewing miles to Broadway in Tarrytown, where the New York State Thruway connection to the Tappan Zee Bridge forces a major intermission on the Aqueduct trail. It is 11 miles to the pond on Broadway in Tarrytown, from Broadway and 242nd Street in Van Cortlandt Park.

METROPOLITAN AREA RUNNING CLUBS

MANHATTAN

Central Park Track Club
c/o David Blackstone
185 East 85th Street
New York, New York 10028
289-4317

Based in Central Park, where almost all of its hundred members train, this club exists only for long-distance competitors. Founded in 1974. Dues are $10 per year.

East Side Track Club
c/o Howard Jacobson
445 East 86th Street
New York, New York 10028
722-8671

Founded in 1977, now has forty-five members. Dues are $10 per year. The club's goal is to support not only running but also racewalking. The club holds free racewalking clinics in Central Park every Saturday at 10:30 A.M. and every Monday at 7 P.M., Ninetieth Street at Fifth Avenue.

Greater New York Athletic Association
c/o Bob Glover Associates
46 West 71st Street, 2-B
New York, New York 10023
580-2310

The G.N.Y.A.A., founded in 1977 to compete in high level races, has sixty male and sixty female members. No dues. The club emphasizes women's running and has won many championships. Prospective members must be proposed by a current member.

Masters Sports Association
11 Park Place
New York, New York 10007
789-6622 (7:30 to 9:30 P.M.)

Sponsors many Masters events. Five hundred members. Dues are $10. per year. Members receive National Masters Newsletter every month.

McBurney Runners Club
215 West 23rd Street
New York, New York 10011
741-9224

Reorganized in 1977, this ninety-member club has no dues. Serves McBurney Y.M.C.A. members who wish to start or to continue running. Training runs leave from the Y lobby.

Metropolitan Amateur Athletic Union
15 Park Row
New York, New York 10038
267-7334

Duenna of amateur athletics in the metropolitan area. Runners must have an A.A.U. number to compete in some New York races, particularly the New York City Marathon. Expect membership processing to take a few months.

New York Athletic Club
180 Central Park South
New York, New York 10019
CI 7-5100

Long-time powerhouse in American distance running.

New York Pioneer Club
c/o 369th Regiment Armory
2366 Fifth Avenue
New York, New York 10037

Founded in 1936 by Joe Yancey, now with two hundred members and annual dues of $12, this is one of the most prestigious clubs in the United States. The Pioneers usually send at least one member to the Olympics. The club believes in promoting understanding and good human relations through track and field.

New York Road Runners Club
Fred Lebow, President
P.O. Box 881
F.D.R. Station
New York, New York 10022
580-6880

An administrative umbrella organization of close to fifteen thousand members who pay annual dues of $10. Organizes and conducts races every weekend of the year throughout the metropolitan area, including the New York City Marathon. Other services for runners include clinics, classes, and access to special materials dealing with running.

92nd Street Y.M.–Y.W.H.A.
1395 Lexington Avenue
New York, New York 10028
427-6000

For Y members only, this Y supports a variety of running programs in heart-disease prevention and rehabilitation and post-mastectomy recovery, among others.

West Side Y.M.C.A. Runners Club
5 West 63rd Street
New York, New York 10023
787-4775

Founded in 1975. Dues $10. a year. A hundred and eighty members, fifty women. About eighty per cent of the members are also members of the West Side Y. Enters teams in road races. This club originated the famous Thursday night Bridge Run to the George Washington Bridge and back.

Vanderbilt Y
224 East 47th Street
New York, New York 10017
755-2410

According to contact Richie Innamorato, this once-active club is now going through a dormant period, with little interest in racing as a team.

BROOKLYN

New York Masters Sports Club
c/o Bob Fine
77 Prospect Place
Brooklyn, New York 11217
789-6622 (between 7:30 and 9:30 P.M.)

A competitive club open to men and women over thirty. Founded in 1979. Dues are $5 a year. Two hundred members. The club supplements keen masters age-group competition with concern for camaraderie and good health.

Prospect Park Track Club
c/o Bob Muller
41 Eastern Parkway
Brooklyn, New York 11238
MA 2-2134

Founded in 1975. $10 dues yearly. A hundred members. Fosters socializing as well as competition. Geared to serving all runners from beginners to serious marathoners.

QUEENS

College Point Athletic Club
P.O. Box 164
College Point, New York 11356

The fifteen club members not only run themselves, but run many age group events.

Flushing Meadow Track Club
c/o Gary Meltzer
134-25 Franklin Avenue
Flushing, New York 11355

The sixty members of the F.M.T.C. encourage all aspects of road running, from family fun runs and marathon training, to hosting the New York 100-Mile Run. Founded in 1977. Dues are $12 per year.

Rockaway Road Runners
c/o Eli Cohan
8403 New Utrecht Avenue
Brooklyn, New York 11214
232-7819

This eighty-member club consists of male and female runners ranging in age from eight to sixty-three. Running purely for recreation, the members help one another to enjoy the sport as much as possible. Founded in 1978. $5 annual dues.

THE BRONX

Bronx Gliders
c/o Joseph Featherstone
2714 Bainbridge Avenue, 4-B
Bronx, New York 10458

Founded in 1978. Fifty members. No dues. The club offers running just for fun in the Fordham-New York Botanical Garden section of the Bronx.

Cahit Pacers Athletic Club
c/o Cahit Yeter
11 Metropolitan Oval, 4-H
Bronx, New York 10462
892-5070

Founded in June 1978, now has more than a hundred members. No dues. Following the pace of Cahit Yeter, this club maintains a marked course through Pelham Bay Park.

Millrose Athletic Association
c/o Joe Kleinerman
2825 Claflin Avenue
Bronx, New York 10468

One of the oldest competitive distance-running clubs in the United States. Only American club ever to win the London-to-Brighton 52.5-mile race. Recently revived a women's team.

Van Cortlandt Track Club
Andy Kimerling, President
P.O. Box 341
Riverdale Station
Bronx, New York 10471

Founded in 1977 to fill the need for another running club in the Bronx. Eighty members, half of them women. Supports all kinds of running from competition to instruction. $10 annual dues.

STATEN ISLAND

North Shore Track Club
c/o Art Hall
290 Myrtle Avenue
Staten Island, New York 10310
273-0988

Thirty members. Founded in 1977. Dues are $15 per year. This club wants only those athletes interested in becoming top-flight road runners.

Staten Island Athletic Club
Bob Orazem, President
P.O. Box 436
Staten Island, New York 10314
981-3037

Two hundred and fifteen members. Dues are $7 a year. Founded in 1966. Club consists of joggers, coaches, sponsors, competitive long-distance runners and track and field athletes. The S.I.A.C. conducts the weekly Saturday clinic and 3-mile fun run in Clove Lakes Park.

LONG ISLAND

Island Track Club
Gary Westerfield, President
P.O. Box 440
Smithtown, Long Island, New York 11707
516-979-7268

A large club, about equally divided between track-and-field and long-distance road runners. The club supports many meets and races in eastern Long Island.

Metropolitan Road Runners Athletic Club
Aldo Scandurra, president
P.O. Box 1046
Port Washington, New York 11050

The two hundred member Metropolitan Road Runners A.C., founded in 1977, recently subdivided itself into two smaller county clubs, Nassau and Suffolk, that will field competitive teams. Sponsors weekly runs. Dues $5.

New Hyde Park Police Boys Club Road Runners
c/o Ed Quinlan
25 Ingraham Lane
New Hyde Park, New York 11040
516-352-4091

In addition to their own training, the club members work to introduce distance running to young boys and girls by conducting numerous age-group competitions.

NEW YORK STATE

Eastchester Road Runners
c/o Jeanne Perlman
36 Stewart Place
Eastchester, New York 10709
914-961-8034

The club's goal is to promote running, especially to help beginners. A hundred members. No dues.

Huguenot Road Runners Club
P.O. Box 1472
New Rochelle, New York 10801
914-235-3276

Formed in 1978. Dues are $8 a year. Seventy-five members. Promotion of community participation in running is of particular concern to the Huguenots.

Scarsdale Antiques
Abe Simon, President for Life
13 Stratton Road
Scarsdale, New York 10583
914-472-0626

No age requirement to be an Antique, but most are in their forties and fifties. No dues, but contributions accepted. The hundred and fifty Antiques aim to dominate the back of the pack. Oldest extant distance running club in Westchester.

Suburban Road Runners Club
P.O. Box 294
Millwood, New York 10546
914-962-9040

Claims to have 1,500 suburban members paying dues of $8 a year.

Taconic Road Runners Club
P.O. Box 99
Baldwin Place, New York 10505

Four hundred members. $10 annual dues. Founded in 1978. Similar to the New York Road Runners Club. The club supports a variety of races including the creative run-and-ski biathlon and the five-distance pentathlon.

Westchester Road Runners Club
Dan Murray, President
P.O. Box 56
Irvington, New York

Founded in 1976, the club now has a hundred members. Dues are $5 per year. The club supports road running in general, with some emphasis on competition.

NEW JERSEY

New Jersey Striders
235 Spring Valley Avenue
Hackensack, New Jersey 07601
201-488-8966

The club sponsors high-school-age-meets, as well as meets for other age groupings in northern New Jersey. Founded in 1978. More than a hundred members. $5 dues per year.

North Jersey Masters Track & Field Club
P.O. Box 56
Ridgewood, New Jersey 07450
201-445-6029

Devoted to competition in masters-class events, most of the three hundred members are over thirty. $5 yearly dues. Founded in 1976. Twenty percent of the members are long-distance runners.

Shore Athletic Club of New Jersey
Elliott Denman, President
28 North Locust Avenue
West Long Branch, New Jersey 07764
201-222-9213

Founded in 1965, a "people's track club." Twelve hundred members. Dues are $7 annually. Promotes the sport of track and field on all levels, in all divisions.

Warren Street Social and Athletic Club
Hugh Sweeny, the Mahatma
212 Warren Street
Jersey City, New Jersey 07302

According to Hugh Sweeny, Warren Street and its runners are in a state of perennial self-transcendence. The W.S.S.A.C. shows up everywhere, is very competitive, both socially and athletically.

ANNUAL ROAD RACES

This selection of races is based on the prestige, uniqueness, or reputation of each run. Only well-established races are mentioned. Unless otherwise noted, write to the New York Road Runners Club, P.O. Box 881, F.D.R. Station, New York, New York 10022, for information and application forms.

JANUARY

WINTER SERIES–B: CENTRAL PARK
Homecoming for many New York runners who decide to continue their summer and autumn jogging into the winter in this two-part series, each composed of a 6-mile and a 10-mile race. Series-A in December, Series-B in January.

SNOWFLAKE MEN'S AND WOMEN'S RUNS: CENTRAL PARK
Separate races for men and women, each of 4 miles. Notorious for poor weather. Course markers and even parts of the course often obliterated by ice and snow. Slow times despite top-flight collegians on vacation.

TACONIC R.R.C. RUN-SKI COMBINE: CLUB BEEKMAN
A unique challenge in this up-country race—run 3 miles and then cross-country ski another 3.

FEBRUARY

FINLANDIA SERIES: CENTRAL PARK
New York Road Runners Club members finishing first, second, and third in this series of three races receive trips to the Finlandia Marathon in Finland, the Peachtree Road Race in Atlanta, and the Falmouth Road Race, respectively. Prizes for men and women.

EMPIRE STATE BUILDING RUN-UP:
Only in N.Y.C.—an eighty-six floor run for those jaded by the usual indoor work-out—1,575 steps, 1,050 feet. By invitation.

N.Y.R.R.C. POSTAL AND MET A.A.U. 15 KILOMETRES: CENTRAL PARK
Simultaneous runs—the local A.A.U. championship and a chance to compare times with road-runners throughout the country who also run a 15-kilometer race on this day, thus the postal.

MIKE HANNON MEMORIAL RUN, 20-MILES: CENTRAL PARK
First indication of who is seriously training for the Boston Marathon.

MARCH

SEVEN MILE REVERSIBLE RUN: CENTRAL PARK
The reversible run has a 3 and a 4-mile loop of Central Park with runners returning to finish in the opposite direction from their start. Unusually fast times, perhaps because of all the hills.

MANUFACTURERS HANOVER BAGEL RUN, 10 KILOMETERS: CENTRAL PARK
The winning team receives a twelve-inch bagel, complete with lox. All other entrants receive smaller pieces.

BLOOMINGDALE'S/PERRIER 10-KILOMETER RUN: CENTRAL PARK
Unofficial start of spring running season in N.Y.C. Huge field full of rookies and fashionably attired runners. East River Jogging Path transposed to Central Park.

MONMOUTH MARATHON: LINDCROFT, N.J.
Last local chance to qualify for the Boston Marathon.

APRIL

COLLEGE POINT HALF–MARATHON: QUEENS
Combines road-running with cross-country in a scenic setting. College Point enthusiastically supports its race.

ROOSEVELT ISLAND 10-km RUN:
No chance to get lost on this course. Two loops along the shore of this historic island. Take the tram over.

EAST SIDE–WEST SIDE 10-km RUN: CENTRAL PARK
Limited by residency requirements, this race has a small field and higher-than-usual places are the reward.

RIVERDALE RAMBLE 7-MILE RUN: BRONX
One of the hilliest, albeit most scenic courses in N.Y.C. Runners enjoy the hospitality of the Van Cortlandt T.C. which uses the course on its weekly training run.

TREVIRA 10-MILE TWOSOME RUN: CENTRAL PARK
Fast men and fast women make up teams in the different age categories. Scoring by couples only. Much maneuvering for partners beforehand. The N.Y.R.R.C. will match runners with partners of similar speed.

TREE BENEFIT RUNS: PROSPECT PARK
The first of a series of four runs (two months apart) featuring novice races of 1 or 2 miles and open races of 5 or 10 kilometers. Entry fees are used by the Friends of Prospect Park to add to and to maintain the park's trees. Contact: Bill Novak, 94 Park Place, Brooklyn, N.Y. 11217.

MAY

STAPLETON STEEPLECHASE: STATEN ISLAND
Designed to support the reclamation efforts of this historic landmark area, the 10-mile course of two loops is the hilliest in N.Y.C. Contact: The Mud Lane Society, P.O. Box 174, Staten Island, N.Y. 10304.

NASSAU COUNTY MARATHON:
The recycled Earth Day Marathon is out-and-back and extremely flat. Good chance for fast times.

YONKERS MARATHON:
The marathoner's marathon. Tortuous hills over the last six miles. Race retains its old-time flavor, perhaps because of the historic course, perhaps because of the small field.

BRONX HISTORICAL SOCIETY 5–MILE RUN: VAN CORTLANDT PARK
Spring cross-country running. A brutal reminder of the rigors of cross-country for road runners.

40–MILE RUN: FOREST PARK, QUEENS
A classy event featuring a famous post race picnic hosted by ultramarathon impresarios Richie In-

namorato and Ben Grundstein. Ten 4-mile loops over a varied terrain.

JUNE

L'EGGS MINI–MARATHON: CENTRAL PARK
Distance now standard at 10 kilometers . The most prestigious womens' running event in the United States. Large field attracts many first time women racers. Great crowds of husbands, children, friends, and spectators urge racers on.

MANUFACTURERS HANOVER CORPORATE CHALLENGE SERIES: CENTRAL PARK
Bring honor and glory to your employer by garnering team laurels. Teams: 5 men, 5 women, or 2 and 2. Separate categories for running-related companies. Three races of 3.5 miles.

NEW YORK 100–MILE RUN:
FLUSHING MEADOW, QUEENS
Top world ultra-marathoners demonstrate the real loneliness of the long-distance runner.

N.Y.R.R.C. BENEFIT RUN, 4 MILES:
CENTRAL PARK
Entry fees donated to a variety of local charities.

JULY

FATHER MOONEY MEMORIAL 8.2–MILE RUN:
MAHOPAC, N.Y.
A Fourth of July fixture. Part of the course is around a beautiful lake, Mahopac. Picnic afterward.

PREFONTAINE MEMORIAL 5 km RUN:
VAN CORTLANDT PARK
Commemorate the late Steve Prefontaine by running his favorite distance.

AUGUST

MANUFACTURERS HANOVER 5–KILOMETRE RUN: PROSPECT PARK
Great course for beginning racers, scenic with one long hill; downhill to tape encourages a finishing kick.

HISPANIC HALF–MARATHON: CENTRAL PARK
The Puerto Rican-Hispanic Sports Association's half-marathon starts the fall season in the park usually on a hot and steamy day. Two park loops with a turn-around after the first half mile.

DIET-PEPSI 10,000 METER SERIES:
CENTRAL PARK
Once around the park for the thin members of the Pepsi Generation.

TACONIC R.R.C. BIATHLON: CLUB BEEKMAN
3 miles on the road ending at a lake shore. Kick off shoes and in you go. First biathlete through the half mile lake course wins the race.

SEPTEMBER

MANUFACTURERS HANOVER HARLEM 10K RUN: 135th STREET
Tour Harlem and Morningside Heights with a large and spirited field. Good crowd. Harlem hospitality.

ATLANTIC ANTIC RUN: BROOKLYN
At 2.5 miles, a good race for beginners. Very competitive field travels the length of Brooklyn's antiques row, but no time for window shopping.

WOMEN'S HALF–MARATHON: CENTRAL PARK
Relatively small field makes this seem like a hometown race. Good prep for the New York City Marathon.

OCTOBER

COLUMBUS DAY RUN: NEW YORK
BOTANICAL GARDEN
3 miles. Two loops of the beautiful inner road of the Garden. Hilly. Tiny field. Contact: New York Center for Ethnic Affairs, 2125 Williamsbridge Road, Bronx, N.Y.

INWOOD HEIGHTS 10-KILOMETER RUN:
BAKER FIELD
Topping both Inwood and Washington Heights, a good quad-tester.

NEW YORK CITY MARATHON:
The ultimate marathon. The people's marathon. A tour of New York's ethnic villages. Every convenience for participants, all 14,000.

10-KILOMETER X-C RUN: VAN CORTLANDT
One of a series of cross country races of varying length over the classic American cross-country course.

NOVEMBER

MET A.A.U. CHAMPIONSHIP, 50 MILES:
CENTRAL PARK
Not necessarily a spectator event, but growing in field and popularity as an annual event on the ultra marathon circuit.

PERRIER WOMEN'S 4–MILE RUN:
CENTRAL PARK
Top field, but short enough distance to encourage novice racers.

R.R.C. OF THE UNITED STATES AGE-GROUP CHAMPIONSHIPS: VAN CORTLANDT PARK
More than four thousand youngsters run a variety of distances. Spend a day at the races.

TURKEY TROT: PROSPECT PARK
Thanksgiving morning: deplete by racing 3.5 miles before the big feed in the afternoon.

DECEMBER

JERSEY SHORE MARATHON: ASBURY PARK
Out-and-back flat course along the Atlantic Ocean. Possible solace for those disappointed with N.Y.C. Marathon time. Cool weather can reduce times. Famous for marathoners finishing race with ice-crusted beards.

WINTER SERIES–A: CENTRAL PARK
Part A of an A and B series, each composed of a 6-mile and a 10-mile race.

NEW YEAR'S EVE MIDNIGHT RUN:
CENTRAL PARK
The best way to ring out the old and ring in the new running year.

RUNNING TRACKS

Tracks are for developing speed and learning race pacing. There are many outdoor tracks in New York City, but only those with public access are listed here. Many schools and colleges have tracks and allow local runners to train on them. Consult school officials for policy.

MANHATTAN

East River Park at East 6th Street, 440 yards, cinder. (Rutted, worn, and poorly maintained; functional rest rooms and fountains.)

(Thomas) Jefferson Park at 112th Street and First Avenue, .21 mile. (Some cinder remains on this narrow track that runs around the ball fields at the south end of the park. For masochistic interval enthusiasts, there is a .20-mile concrete track littered with broken glass at the north end of the park; working rest rooms and fountains.)

Randall's Island—John J. Downing Stadium 440 yards, all-weather track. (The best public track in the city, soft surface, yet firm. Available only to groups that have obtained a permit. Hot showers for competitors; lighted at night.)

Riverside Park at Riverside Drive and West 74th Street, 220 yards, cinder. (A heavily used and fairly well-maintained track.)

BROOKLYN

Betsy Head Memorial Playground at Hopkinson and Dumont Avenues, 440 yards, cinder. (Dilapidated, but used by neighborhood regulars.)

Red Hook Recreational Area Stadium at Bay and Columbia Streets, 440 yards, cinder. (Fair condition, heavily used, especially by high school teams.)

McCarren Park Driggs Avenue between Lorimer and North 12th Streets, 440 yards, cinder. (Heavily used by neighborhood runners. Well-worn inside lane, no shade.)

QUEENS

Astoria Park 18th Street and Astoria Park South, 440 yards, cinder. (Fair repair, heavily used; working fountains and solar-heated showers available.)

Forest Park—Victory Field at Myrtle Avenue and Woodhaven Boulevard, 440 yards, cinder. (Site of high school meets, intact rest rooms and fountains. Hot showers in administration building on Woodhaven Boulevard when the boiler is working.)

Juniper Valley Park—Brennan Field Juniper Boulevard South and 74th Street, Middle Village, 440 yards, cinder. (Rarely used due to washout of 30 yards of track at south end.)

Liberty Park Liberty Avenue and 172nd Street, Jamaica, 440 yards, cinder. (Some neighborhood use, but rutted and overgrown.)

BRONX

Macomb's Dam Park at River Street and East 161st Street, 440 yards, cinder. (Set in the shadow of Yankee Stadium, beneath the roar of the El, this track is heavily used by the neighborhood. Good repair, but no working facilities as a result of vandalism.)

Pelham Bay Park—Rice Stadium 440 yards, cinder. (Good condition, used by neighborhood and the Cahit Pacers for speed workouts. No lights, but working rest rooms and fountains.)

Van Cortlandt Park Stadium at Broadway and 241st Street, 440 yards, cinder. (Site of high-school meets, inside lane rutted, floods after heavy rain.)

INDOOR RUNNING TRACKS

This list includes only those indoor tracks available to the public free or for a nominal daily fee. Many colleges and private clubs in New York have indoor or covered tracks. Access, however, is restricted to members or institutional personnel.

Indoor running is a pursuit only for those days when running outdoors is unthinkable. Besides the terminal boredom of innumerable laps, surfaces are often hard, banked, and sharp-cornered. Too much indoor running of this sort can lead to injury.

Call ahead to ensure that the track you choose is open, and to determine cost, presence of lockers, and availability of other amenities.

(Outdoor Running Tracks continued)

Williamsbridge Playground at East 208th Street and Bainbridge Avenue, 440 yards, cinder. (Fair repair, used by neighborhood runners.)

STATEN ISLAND

Great Kills Park at Hylan Boulevard and Great Kills, 440 yards, cinder. (Neglected and weedy.)

MANHATTAN

McBurney Y.M.C.A. 215 West 23rd Street, 741-9224. (20 laps per mile; rubberized mat.)

92nd Street Y.M.–Y.W.H.A. 1395 Lexington Avenue, 427-6000. (32 laps per mile; rubberized mat.)

Parks and Recreation Department Gymnasium Seventh Avenue at Clarkson and Carmine Streets, 397-3147. (32 laps per mile; cork.) The building has been under renovation, so call to make sure the track is available.

Parks and Recreation Department Gymnasium 134th Street between Lenox and Fifth Avenues, 397-3193. (35 laps per mile; cork.)

Vanderbilt Y.M.C.A. 224 East 47th Street, 755-2410. (No track, but 28 laps of the gym's perimeter make a mile; hardwood.)

West Side Y.M.C.A. 5 West 63rd Street, 787-4400. (24 laps per mile; rubberized mat.)

BROOKLYN

Brooklyn Y.W.C.A.–Downtown Brooklyn Athletic Club 30 Third Avenue at Atlantic Avenue, 875-1190. (28 laps per mile; rubberized mat.)

Prospect Park–Bay Ridge Y.M.C.A. 9th Street and Sixth Avenue, 768-7100. (32 (28 laps per mile; rubberized mat.)

STATEN ISLAND

Cromwell Center Pier 6, Tompkinsville, Staten Island, 442-8979. (200-meter track around hardwood basketball floor.)

Staten Island Y.M.C.A. 651 Broadway, 981-4933. (No track, but two gyms, one 18 and the other 25 laps per mile; hardwood.)

NEW YORK CITY RUNNING RULES

1. STREETS AND SIDEWALKS

It is always safest to run on the sidewalk. Before crossing a street, look carefully *both* ways. Do not run red lights. *STOP*, stretch or relax. Never presume that cars will look out for you. In a showdown, yield to cars or bicycles—they move faster than runners and cannot stop as easily. If running in the street, always run facing traffic. Be alert for cars pulling out from the curb and for doors flung open. Don't run beside diesel routes or roads with heavy stop-and-go traffic; avoid their higher levels of carbon monoxide and lead inhalation. Because of lighter traffic on the roads, Sundays, holidays, and very early weekday mornings are the least polluted times for city running. On turtlebacked roads (most in the city are) reverse direction occasionally so that right and left legs get equal workouts. Be on the lookout for potholes, raised-metal gas caps, emergent antique trolley tracks, and cobbled streets. You may run across or beside railroad tracks, keep watch for trains. Do not touch electrified rails.

2. PARKS

Avoid isolated areas unless running with a partner or a group. (A running dog large enough to attack a mugger or rapist is also a strong deterrent.) If you know that a certain route is crowded with strollers or bicyclists on weekend afternoons, run it early or run it late. Barging through crowds is frustrating and ruins your rhythm. Exhibitionists are a not uncommon part of park life; they are generally harmless and can be ignored. Finish your run and then report the sighting to the police.

3. RAPE

Rapists in runners' clothing, as well as in civvies, go after women runners, and any woman who runs should be aware of that. Close to four thousand rapes are reported in New York City each year, (twenty-nine occurred in Central Park in 1977), and, according to police statistics, rapes occur most often in July, August, and September—prime running months—between 8 P.M. and 5 A.M.

Rapists rely on the element of surprise, and, according to the police department, your "presence" has a lot to do with whether or not a rapist will bother to attack you. Look strong, assertive, in command, and be aware of your surroundings. Keep track of people on and off the road behind, beside, and ahead of you. Awareness of your surroundings is as important to safe running as are proper stride and breathing. Don't daydream. Dress defensively—that is, keep fairly well covered, wear standard running gear (not bikinis or chichi hotpants) and wear a bra as another element of self-protection. Don't count on men running nearby to be watching out for you or to notice if you are in trouble. Often they are running in a private world. Women who run alone should avoid isolated areas and ought to carry a chemical spray such as ammonia (or vinegar or lemon juice) or position their set of keys between the fingers of one hand, points out, to make brass knuckles. If you are attacked, scream if that is possible, and if it makes sense hit him in a "devastation area"—the eyes, Adam's apple, solar plexus, groin, shin, kneecap, or instep—then run like hell and report the attack to the police, immediately. (The Police Department's Rape Help Line is 233-3000.) A self-protective weapon is not recommended, as the attacker could disarm you and use it against you. There is greater safety in running-numbers than in any other preventive act.

4. MUGGINGS

Muggers are sometimes dumb enough to go after runners. Give them the chronograph—most likely the only item of value you will have with you. Use your common sense in choosing a route. Do not run close to bushes, masses of trees, or empty lots where you can be jumped.

5. WEATHER

Pay attention to the weather report. Do not run during electrical storms. If caught during one, especially if you are in the middle of a large field, lie down. Don't be a lightning rod. Don't decide to run across a bridge or beside the ocean during high winds or heavy rains. Take into account the wind-chill factor—that it's generally cooler by the ocean and that unexpected temperature drops occur. Carry a windbreaker for such times. In the winter months and in early spring, hypothermia is a possibility in exposed places. After rains, watch out for mud slicks and erosion.

In winter be extremely cautious on snow and ice, which can cause you to pull ligaments and tendons. Run with attention and slow down—do the distance or a reasonable portion of it. Avoid salted areas as salt eats shoes. Wear a wool cap, mittens, and long johns to conserve body heat, and remember that frostbite can occur. It is especially dangerous for men to wear nylon running shorts and nylon underwear in sleet and freezing rain. Wool undergarments and sweatpants are required.

On hot summer days, it's best not to run at high noon, but to run either early or late. If you choose to run in the sun, wear a hat or visor, shades, and sun block and carry a wet sponge or wrap a wet, iced bandanna around your hand. If water stops are uncertain, carry a plastic-straw bottle (though in New York there is usually a deli or corner grocery nearby). Be sensible about hot weather running, underdo rather than overdo and risk heat prostration. On days when the air is stagnant and there is a pollution alert, you might be better off to ruminate in place, instead of running.

6. DARK AND DAWN

At night and before it is fully daylight, wear light-reflectors or light colors so that you can be seen. Do not run in the road at night. In winter, both at night and at dawn, it is very hard to see black ice. Run only well-lighted places and in nonhostile areas. Be sensible about where it is safe to run alone at night, especially women runners. Don't put yourself in danger.

7. DOGS

Should a dog go for you, stop. Face it, then pick up a stone and hurl it.

127

Shout "No!" (Yell at the owner to releash his beast.) Do not turn your back. In some areas, packs of wild dogs collect over the summer when people abandon their pets in the parks. Over the past few years dog packs have been sighted in Prospect, Central, and Inwood Hill Parks.

8. IN GENERAL

When a park is described as "safe" it is not a guarantee that rock-throwing kids, or kids exercising slingshots or firecrackers or golf clubs won't show up there, along with rapists or muggers. What's safe is what has generally been found to be so over the years, and is relative to areas that are always thought to be "unsafe" like Crown Heights or the South Bronx. It all depends on who happens to be where, when.

Practice preventive running. Tape your predictable blister spots before you go out, and carry moleskin. Take a dollar and an I.D. with you. Don't carry valuables. Have an idea where you can find water and rest rooms along the way.

In short, think out your route ahead of time, study the route maps, and be alert. Don't daydream or get into the much-touted runners high. Knowledge of the course is your best guarantee against problems. And the buddy system helps too. For city running you need your wits about you at all times. And remember that in running, at least, it is often possible to run away from problems.

Patti Hagan is on the staff of *The New Yorker* magazine and usually races in the company T-shirt. She has written for *The New Yorker, The New York Times*, the *Washington Post, The Village Voice, Ms., Saturday Review.*

She was graduated from Stanford University before *Runner's World* moved in down the road from campus, and so missed the chance to take up even a mild form of undergraduate running. In 1973, she became a miler for the health and exercise of her golden retriever, Thurber. Upon finding a second golden retriever while out running one day, she upped her regular distance to two miles, on behalf of Petunia. Two years ago she was entered—against her noncompetitive instincts—in a 2.5-mile race. More races of greater length followed. Having watched her first marathon in October, 1977, she ran her first marathon on October 22, 1978, the New York City. She lives in Prospect Heights, Brooklyn, and aspires to become a borough-class runner.

Although she comes from Seattle, she considers herself an adoptive New Yorker, by now thoroughly unfit to live anywhere else. Prior to her incarnation as a runner she enjoyed hiking, mountain climbing, bicycling, sailing, and swimming.

Joe Cody is a teacher at Horace Mann School in the Bronx. He was a varsity football player at Columbia, a member of the Old Blue rugby team, and an all-around athlete who took up running in 1977, and completed the New York City Marathon in 1978. He lives in Yonkers.